An Orange Tree Theatre production

CHURCHILL IN MOSCOW

by HOWARD BRENTON

This play was first performed on 3 February 2025
at the Orange Tree Theatre, Richmond.

A powerhouse of independent theatre

CAST

Winston Churchill **Roger Allam**
Archie Clark Kerr **Alan Cox**
Vyacheslav Molotov **Julius D'Silva**
Joseph Stalin **Peter Forbes**
Svetlana Stalin **Tamara Greatrex**
Sally Powell **Jo Herbert**
Olga Dovzhenko **Elisabeth Snegir**

CREATIVES AND PRODUCTION TEAM

Writer **Howard Brenton**
Director **Tom Littler**
Designer **Cat Fuller**
Lighting Designer **Johanna Town**
Sound Designer & Composer **Max Pappenheim**
Associate Sound Designer **Anna Wood**
Movement Director **Julia Cave**
Casting Director **Matilda James CDG**
Voice & Dialect Coach **Nick Trumble**
Costume Supervisor **Evelien Van Camp**
Wigs Supervisor & Hair Stylist **Chris Smyth**
Hair & Makeup Consultant for Roger Allam **Vicky Voller**
Hair & Makeup for Roger Allam **Amy Richardson**
Assistant Director **Rosie Tricks**
Cultural Consultant & Translator **Olga Utrivanova**
Production Photographer **Tristram Kenton**

Company Stage Manager **Jade Gooch**
Deputy Stage Manager **Megan Smith**
Assistant Stage Manager **Judith Volk**

Production Manager **Gemma Brooks**
Production & Technical Director **Phil Bell**
Production Electrician **Chris Galler**
Scenic Artists **Anita Gander, Emma Turner** and **Sophie Firth**
Production Technician **Andy Cook**
Production Technician **Priya Virdee**

ROGER ALLAM
Winston Churchill

Roger is a multi-award-winning actor who has performed extensively in the West End, the National Theatre and RSC where he is an Associate Artist.

Theatre credits include: *Frank and Percy* (Theatre Royal Windsor, The Other Palace); *A Number* (Bridge Theatre); *Rutherford and Sons* (National Theatre); *Limehouse* (Donmar Warehouse); *The Moderate Soprano* (Hampstead Theatre, West End); *Seminar* (Hampstead Theatre); *The Tempest* (Globe Theatre); *Uncle Vanya* (Chichester Festival Theatre); *Henry IV Parts I & II* (Globe Theatre, Olivier Award); *La Cage Aux Folles* (West End); *God of Carnage* (Theatre Royal Bath); *Afterlife* (National Theatre); *The Giant* (Hampstead Theatre); *Boeing Boeing* (Comedy Theatre); *Pravda* (Chichester Festival Theatre); *Aladdin* (Old Vic); *City of Angels* (West End, Olivier Award Nomination), *Democracy* (West End, Olivier Award Nomination); *Privates on Parade* (Donmar Warehouse, Olivier Award); *The Cherry Orchard* (National Theatre); *Summerfolk* (National Theatre, Olivier Award Nomination) and *Money* (National Theatre, Olivier Award). He created the role of Javert in *Les Miserables,* and played Adolf Hitler in *Albert Speer* (National Theatre).

Film credits include: *The Choral, Tetris, Say Your Prayers, The Hippopotamus, The Truth Commissioner, The Lady in the Van, Mr. Holmes, A Royal Night Out, The Book Thief, The Angels Share, The Iron Lady, The Woman in Black, Pirates of the Caribbean: On Stranger Tides, Tamara Drewe, Speed Racer, The Queen, The Wind that Shakes the Barley,* and *V for Vendetta*.

Television credits include: *The Sandman, Murder in Provence, Endeavour S1-9, The Missing, Parade's End, The Jury, Game of Thrones, Ashes to Ashes, Margaret, The Curse of Steptoe, The Thick of It, Spooks, Meet the Robinsons, Inspector Lynley, Manchild,* and *Foyle's War.*

Radio appearances include: *Conversations from a Long Marriage, Cabin Pressure, How Does That Make You Feel?* and *The Government Inspector.*

ALAN COX
Archie Clark Kerr

Orange Tree Theatre credits include: *The Dark River*, *The Daughter in Law*.

Theatre credits include: *Farm Hall*, *The Importance of Being Earnest* (Theatre Royal Haymarket); *My Fair Lady*, *The King's Speech* (Frinton Summer Theatre); *Take The Rubbish Out, Sasha, But It Still Goes On*, *Cornelius* (Finborough Theatre); *Love All* (Jermyn Street Theatre); *Uncle Vanya* (Hampstead Theatre); *Hamlet* (Shakespeare Theatre of Washington); *Opening Skinner's Box* (West Yorkshire Playhouse); *Forty Years On*, *The Lady's Not for Burning* (Chichester Festival Theatre); *The Divided Laing* (Arcola Theatre); *Frost/Nixon* (US Tour); *The Earthly Paradise* (Almeida Theatre); *An Enemy of the People*, *Absolute Hell*, *The Seagull* (National Theatre); *The Winter's Tale*, *Antony and Cleopatra*, *As You Like It*, *The Beggar's Opera* (RSC).

Film and television credits include: *Dante*, *Magic Mike's Last Dance*, *Say My Name*, *Before We Go*, *The Dictator*, *Contagion*, *Not Only But Always*, *Cor Blimey*, *Mrs Dalloway*, *Young Sherlock Holmes*, *New Amsterdam*, *The Good Wife*, *Lucan*, *MI High*, *The Wild West: Custer's Last Stand*, *Housewife 49*, *Mrs David*, *Midsomer Murders*, *Dinosaur Hunters*, *The Odyssey*.

JULIUS D'SILVA
Vyacheslav Molotov

Theatre credits include: *Farm Hall* (Theatre Royal Haymarket, Theatre Royal Bath & Jermyn Street Theatre); *& Juliet* (Shaftesbury Theatre & Regent Theatre, Melbourne); *What's New Pussycat?* (Birmingham Rep); *The Producers* (Manchester Royal Exchange); *The Cherry Orchard* (Bristol Old Vic / Manchester Royal Exchange); *Strictly Ballroom* (West Yorkshire Playhouse & Toronto); *Made in Dagenham* (Adelphi Theatre); *Eternal Love*; *Anne Boleyn* (Shakespeare's Globe / ETT / UK Tour); *Macbeth* (Shakespeare's Globe); *Oliver!* (Theatre Royal Drury Lane); *Aristo* (Chichester Festival Theatre); *Henry IV Parts 1 & 2*, *Henry V*, *Henry VI Parts 1-3*, *Richard III* (The Royal Shakespeare Company); *Great Expectations* (RSC / Cheek By Jowl); *Dog in the Manger*; *Tamar's Revenge*, *House of Desires*, and *Pedro The Great Pretender* (RSC); *The Wax King* (LSW); *As You Like It* (BAC); *The Importance of Being Earnest* (Insomniac Limited); *Tess of the D'Urbervilles* (Greenwich Studio); *The Tempest* (Edinburgh Festival); *Noises Off* (Gallery Productions); *Vergil and Caesar* (Oxford Playhouse); *Bouncers* (Burton Taylor Theatre); and *Richard II* (Ludlow Festival, directed by Steven Berkoff).

Film and television credits include: *Notes on a Scandal*, *Full Circle*, *Endgame*, *Bridgerton*, *The Crown*, *The Ten Commandments*, *How We Used to Live: Spanish Armada*, and *Highlander*.

For BBC Radio 4: *Jude the Obscure*, *Wordsworth and Coleridge: The Lyrical Ballads*, *The Flea* by John Donne, *The Horse* by Rana Dasgupta, and *Van Gogh: The Letters*.

PETER FORBES
Joseph Stalin

Orange Tree Theatre credits include: *Winner Takes All*, *A Journey to London* and *Adam Bede*.

Theatre credits include: *Coriolanus*, *Jack Absolute Flies Again*, *Follies*, *Our Country's Good*, *The Observer*, *Afterlife*, *Never So Good*, *Two Weeks With The Queen* (National Theatre); *The James Plays*, *Black Watch* (National Theatre of Scotland); *Singin' in the Rain*, *Mamma Mia!*, *Henceforward...* (West End), *Allelujah!* (Bridge Theatre); *How To Hold Your Breath* (Royal Court); *The Same Deep Water as Me* (Donmar Warehouse); *The Winter's Tale*, *Troilus & Cressida* (Shakespeare's Globe); *My Dad's A Birdman* (Young Vic); *La Cage Aux Folles*, *A Midsummer Night's Dream*, *Twelfth Night*, *A Funny Thing Happened on the Way to the Forum*, *The Comedy of Errors*, *The Tempest* (Regent's Park); *Assassins*, *Way Upstream*, *A Small Family Business*, *A Word From Our Sponsor* (Chichester Festival Theatre); *The Scent of Roses*, *A Number*, *Educating Agnes* (Royal Lyceum, Edinburgh); *The Contingency Plan* (Sheffield Theatres); *A Christmas Carol: A Ghost Story* (Nottingham Playhouse / Alexandra Palace); *Cat on a Hot Tin Roof* (ETT / Leicester Curve).

Television credits include: *Traces* (Alibi / BBC); *Towards Zero*, *Poldark*, *EastEnders*, *Casualty*, *Holby City*, *Doctors*, *The First Men in the Moon*, *Berkeley Square* (BBC); *Stephen*, *Manhunt*, *Victoria*, *Endeavour*, *Little Devil*, *Bad Girls*, *The Bill*, *A Touch of Frost*, *Taggart* (ITV); *King Lear* (Amazon), *The Crown* (Netflix), *The Promise*, *The Government Inspector*, *The English Revolution* (Channel 4), *Walking on the Moon* (United Film and Television Productions); *The Stalker's Apprentice* (Scottish Television).

Film credits include: *Judy* (Pathe); *The Children Act* (BBC Films); *The Wife* (Anonymous Content); *Modern Life is Rubbish* (Serotonin Films); *Nativity 3: Dude, Where's My Donkey?* (Mirrorball Films); *Wilde* (Samuelson Entertainments); *Blue Ice*.

JO HERBERT

Sally Powell

Theatre credits include: *Dear Octopus* (National Theatre), directed by Emily Burns, and *The Southbury Child* (Bridge Theatre), directed by Nicholas Hytner.

Jo has played major roles at the National Theatre, Chichester Festival Theatre, Hampstead Theatre and at the Globe Theatre, working with such esteemed directors as Simon Godwin and Howard Davies.

Television credits include: *Call the Midwife*, *Unforgotten*, *The Crown*, *Grace*, *Home Fires*.

Film credits include: *Misbehaviour* (Pathe), directed by Phillipa Lowthorpe.

ELISABETH SNEGIR

Olga Dovzhenko

Theatre credits include: *Mozart – Her Story* (Theatre Royal Drury Lane), *In & Out of Chekhov's Shorts* (Southwark Playhouse), *The Anarchist* (Jermyn Street Theatre), *A Christmas Carol: The Haunted Service* (Goblin Theatre Co), *The Scarlet Letter* (The Actors Church, Covent Garden) and *Father Christmas at the Hall* (Royal Albert Hall).

Film credits include: *Ebony Rose* and *Blown*.

Television credits include: *Midnight at the Pera Palace* (voice of Sonia – Seasons 1 & 2, Netflix).

TAMARA GREATREX

Svetlana Stalin

Churchill in Moscow is Tamara's professional theatre debut.

Film and television credits include: *Calico*, *In Eva: Stories*.

Tamara trained at ArtsEd and National Youth Theatre.

HOWARD BRENTON
Writer

Howard Brenton was born in 1942. He began to write for the emerging fringe theatre in the late 1960s, the Royal Court made him Writer In Residence in 1973 and he went on to write for many theatres, among them the RSC, National Theatre, Shakespeare's Globe, and The Hampstead Theatre. His many plays include *Magnificence* at The Royal Court (1973); *Epsom Downs* for Joint Stock Theatre (1977); *The Romans in Britain* at the National Theatre (1980); *Thirteenth* at the RSC (1981); *Bloody Poetry* for Foco Novo (1983) revived by The Royal Court (1987); *Pravda* at The National Theatre (1985, written with David Hare) and *Berlin Bertie* at The Royal Court (1992).

Plays this century include *Paul* (2005), *Never So Good* (2008) and a version of Buchner's *Danton's Death* (2010) at the National Theatre; *In Extremis* (2008), *Anne Boleyn* (2010) and *Doctor Scroggy's War* (2014) at Shakespeare's Globe; *55 Days* (2012), *The Arrest of Ai Weiwei* (2013), *Drawing the Line* (2013) and *Lawrence After Arabia* (2016) at Hampstead Theatre; *The Shadow Factory* (2018) at Southampton's Nuffield Theatre and *Cancelling Socrates* at the Jermyn Street Theatre (2022).

When Artistic Director at the Jermyn Street Theatre, Tom Littler asked Brenton to explore the work of August Strindberg and he wrote *The Blinding Light* (2017), about Strindberg's 'Inferno' crisis, and versions of *Miss Julie* (2017) and *Creditors* (2019).

TOM LITTLER
Director

Tom has been Artistic Director of the Orange Tree since late 2022. At the OT, Tom has directed *The Circle* by Somerset Maugham (remounted for a national tour by Theatre Royal Bath); Oliver Goldsmith's *She Stoops to Conquer*; Noël Coward's *Suite in Three Keys* (also at Theatre Royal Bath); and William Shakespeare's *Twelfth Night*.

Tom has directed over seventy productions across the UK and Europe. *Churchill in Moscow* is his seventh collaboration with Howard Brenton. He has directed the world premieres of *Cancelling Socrates* and *The Blinding Light* (Jermyn Street Theatre), three new versions of plays by Strindberg, *Miss Julie* and *Creditors* (Jermyn Street Theatre and Theatre by the Lake) and *Dances of Death* (Gate Theatre), and a revival of *Bloody Poetry* (Jermyn Street Theatre).

He has collaborated with contemporary writers including Lorna French, Natalie Haynes, Charlotte Jones, Hannah Khalil, Bryony Lavery, Isley Lynn, Joanna Murray-Smith, Lucy Shaw, Timberlake Wertenbaker and Alexandra Wood. He has directed several musicals, especially by Stephen Sondheim. Revivals include Noël Coward's nine play *Tonight at 8.30* cycle (Jermyn

Street Theatre), and work by Alan Ayckbourn, Alan Bennett, Jean-Jacques Bernard, T.S. Eliot, August Strindberg, Keith Waterhouse, and the first ever revivals of plays by Graham Greene, Dorothy L. Sayers, Terence Rattigan, and Charles Wood.

Tom's theatre-on-screen work includes *15 Heroines* for Jermyn Street Theatre and Digital Theatre (OffWestEnd Award), and *The Odyssey* (OffWestEnd Award).

Tom was Artistic Director and Executive Producer of Jermyn Street Theatre from 2017 to 2022, during which he won the OffWestEnd Award for Best Artistic Director, and the theatre won The Critics' Circle Award for Exceptional Theatre Making During Lockdown and The Stage Award. Previously, Tom was Artistic Director of Primavera, Associate Director of Theatre503, and Associate Director of the Peter Hall Company. He has ten OffWestEnd Award nominations for Best Director.

Tom trained as an assistant and associate to directors including Peter Gill, Peter Hall, and Trevor Nunn. He read English at the University of Oxford and has postgraduate degrees from the Open University and the University of Cambridge, where he subsequently taught eighteenth-century literature.

CAT FULLER
Designer

Cat Fuller has an MA in Performance Design from Bristol Old Vic Theatre School. In 2021 Cat was named a recipient of the Linbury Prize and was also awarded the John Elvery Prize for Excellence in Stage Design.

Orange Tree Theatre credits include: *Red Speedo* (costume designer and associate set designer) and *Testmatch* (Co-production with ETT & Octagon Theatre).

Her recent work as set and costume designer includes: *The Maids* (Jermyn Street Theatre & Reading Rep), *Scarlet Sunday* (Omnibus Theatre), *Owners* (Jermyn Street Theatre), *Flies* (Shoreditch Town Hall), *Snail* (VAULT), *The Sweet Science of Bruising* (The Egg, Theatre Royal Bath); *Romeo and Juliet* (Weston Studio, Bristol Old Vic). Work as set designer includes *The Three Seagulls* (Bristol Old Vic); and *Falling in Love Again* (The King's Head). Her work as Associate Designer for Anna Fleischle includes: *The Time Traveller's Wife: The Musical* (Apollo Theatre London & Chester Storyhouse), *A Christmas Carol* (Finnish National Opera and Ballet), *Home, I'm Darling* (UK Tour), and *Much Ado About Nothing* (National Theatre); and for Katie Sykes: *If You Fall* (Theatre Ad Infinitum).

JOHANNA TOWN
Lighting Designer

Johanna Town is the Chair of the Association for Lighting Production and Design and a Fellow of Guildhall School of Music & Drama.

Orange Tree Theatre credits include: *Uncle Vanya*.

Her theatre credits include: *Vardy v Rooney: The Wagatha Christie Trial* (West End / UK Tour), *Two Ladies* (Bridge Theatre), *The Tempest*, *Don Quixote* (RSC), *The Sound of Music*, *The Famous Five*, *The Butterfly Lion*, *The Watsons*, *The Norman Conquests*, *Fracked* (Chichester Festival Theatre), *Play On The Musical* (Talawa Theatre / UK Tour), *Fisherman's Friends The Musical* (UK Tour / Canada), *Identical* (Kenny Wax / Nottingham Playhouse), *Some Like It Hip Hop* (ZooNation UK Tour), *The Score*, *The Homecoming* (Theatre Royal Bath & UK Tour), *The Lightest Element*, *Peggy For You*, *The Memory of Water*, *The Death of a Black Man* (Hampstead Theatre), *Brainstorming*, *Moon on a Rainbow Shawl*, *The Permanent Way* (National Theatre), *The Importance of Being Earnest*, *Guys and Dolls*, *Queen Margaret*, *Frankenstein*, *The House of Bernarda Alba* (Royal Exchange, Manchester), *The Habit of Art*, *Being Mr Wickham* (Original Theatre Company / 59e59, New York), *The Hypochondriac*, *Paper*, *Rutherford and Son*, *Love and Information*, *Julius Caesar* (Sheffield Crucible), *Miss Julie*, *Creditors* (Jermyn Street Theatre).

Her opera credits include: *The Queen of Spades*, *Orfeo ed Euridice*, *Dido and Aeneas*, *Cosi Fan Tutte*, *Tamerlano* (The Grange); *Porgy and Bess* (Royal Danish Opera); *Rinaldo* (Estonian National Opera); *Carmen*, *Katya Kabanova*, *The Secret Marriage* (Scottish Opera).

MAX PAPPENHEIM
Sound Designer & Composer

Orange Tree Theatre credits include: *Uncle Vanya*, *Humble Boy*, *Blue/Heart* and *The Distance*.

Recent theatre includes: *The Night of the Iguana*, *Cruise* (West End); *The School for Scandal*, *Crooked Dances* (Royal Shakespeare Company); *Coram Boy*, *Macbeth* (Chichester Festival Theatre); *Twelfth Night* (Regent's Park Open Air Theatre); *A Raisin in the Sun* (Headlong); *Shed: Exploded View* (Royal Exchange); *A Doll's House, Part 2*, *The Way of the World* (Donmar Warehouse); *The Invention of Love*, *The Divine Mrs S*, *Nineteen Gardens*, *Blackout Songs*, *Linck and Mülhahn*, *Labyrinth* (Hampstead Theatre); *Village Idiot*, *One Night in Miami* (Nottingham Playhouse); *Henry V* (Shakespeare's Globe / Headlong); *Hamlet* (Bristol Old Vic); *The Children* (also Broadway), *Ophelias Zimmer* (Royal Court); *Feeling Afraid As If Something Terrible Is Going To Happen*, *Old Bridge* (Bush

Theatre); *The Homecoming*, *My Cousin Rachel* (Theatre Royal Bath); *The Syndicate*, *Murder in the Dark*, *The Mirror Crack'd*, *Wish You Were Dead*, *The Circle*, *Looking Good Dead* (National Tours).

Opera and Ballet includes: *The Limit* (Royal Ballet); *The Marriage of Figaro* (Salzburg Festival); *Miranda* (Opéra Comique, Paris); *Hansel and Gretel* (BYO / Opera Holland Park); *Scraww* (Trebah Gardens). Online includes *The System*, *Barnes' People*, *The Haunting of Alice Bowles* (Original Theatre); *15 Heroines* (Digital Theatre). Associate Artist of Orange Tree Theatre, The Faction and Silent Opera.

Awards include: OffWestEnd Award for Sound Design for *Old Bridge*.

ANNA WOOD
Associate Sound Designer

Theatre credits include: *A Streetcar Named Desire* (Almeida Theatre); *Romeo and Juliet* (Cambridge Arts Theatre); *Laughing Boy* (Jermyn Street Theatre / Theatre Royal Bath); *Sam Wu Is Not Afraid of Ghosts* (Polka Theatre); *I Really Do Think This Will Change Your Life* (Mercury Theatre). Anna trained as a composer at the Royal Welsh College of Music and Drama.

JULIA CAVE
Movement Director

Training: Mountview.

Orange Tree Theatre credits include: *Twelfth Night* and *She Stoops To Conquer*.

Theatre credits as Choreographer and Movement Director include: *Cinderella* and *A Midsummer Night's Dream* (Chichester Festival Theatre); *The Smeds and The Smoos* (UK, International tour and West End); *Around The World in 80 Days* (Devonshire Park); *Peter and The Wolf* (Waterperry Opera Festival / Opera Holland Park); Hamlet (Guildford Shakespeare Company); *Twelfth Night* (East London Shakespeare Festival); *The Tempest* (Jermyn Street); *Treasure Island* (Octagon Theatre Bolton); *The Children*, *Home*, *I'm Darling*, *Pride and Prejudice*, *Sleeping Beauty*, *Goodnight Mr Tom*, *Treasure Island*, *Our Day Out*, *Arabian Nights*, *Dick Whittington*, *Beauty and the Beast*, *Jack and the Beanstalk* and *Cinderella* (Theatre Royal Bury St Edmunds); *Pictures of Dorian Gray* (Stephen Joseph / Jermyn Street / Blackwell's Oxford); *Wizard of Oz* (Salisbury Playhouse); *The Importance of Being Earnest*, *Othello*, *A Midsummer Night's Dream*, *Nell Gywnn* and *The Winter's Tale* (Changeling Theatre); *Lord of The Flies* (Greenwich Theatre); *Infinite Joy* (Southwark Playhouse); *Northanger Abbey* (UK Tour); *The Picture of Dorian Gray* (English Theatre Frankfurt);

Stig of The Dump (UK tour and West End); Clown-Hearted (Vaults Festival); Taming of The Shrew (Brockley Jack); King Lear (The Space); Women Of Troy (Blue Elephant).

Julia has also choreographed many musicals for National Youth Music Theatre, British Youth Music Theatre, and a number of drama schools. She has also directed numerous pantomimes all over the UK.

MATILDA JAMES CDG
Casting Director

Originally from Cornwall, Matilda works in casting for theatre, screen, and games. As Casting Director at Shakespeare's Globe from 2012-2017, she cast over 50 shows for the Globe and Sam Wanamaker Playhouse. A founding member of The Murmuration, a women-led theatre and arts producing collective, her recent collaborations include work with the Barbican, York Theatre Royal and Kyiv City Ballet, #Merky Films, and Citizens of the World, the UK's leading choir for people seeking sanctuary and asylum.

Orange Tree Theatre credits include: Twelfth Night, Guards at the Taj, Here in America, Red Speedo, Suite in Three Keys, Testmatch, Uncle Vanya and Northanger Abbey.

Other theatre credits include: Reverberation (Bristol Old Vic); The Cat and the Canary (Chichester Festival Theatre, Told by an Idiot); The History Boys (Bath Theatre Royal); A Child of Science (Bristol Old Vic); The House Party (Chichester Festival Theatre, Headlong Theatre); QUIZ (Wessex Grove, JCTP); 2.22 A Ghost Story (West End and on tour); Family Tree (Actors Touring Company, Belgrade Theatre Coventry, Brixton House) and Gin Craze! (Northampton Royal & Derngate, English Touring Theatre).

TV and Film credits include: Portraits of Dangerous Women, Benjamin and Pond Life.

NICK TRUMBLE
Voice & Dialect Coach

Received an MA in Voice Studies from The Royal Central School of Speech & Drama.

Orange Tree Theatre credits include: Suite in Three Keys and She Stoops to Conquer.

Theatre credits include: Mary Poppins (Prince Edward Theatre & UK Tour), The Importance of Being Earnest (Grosvenor Park), Player Kings (Noël Coward Theatre), Lemons Lemons Lemons Lemons Lemons (Garrick Theatre), As You Like It (@sohoplace), Sweet Charity (Donmar Warehouse), Funny Girl (Savoy Theatre), Aladdin (Prince Edward Theatre), The Price (Theatre Royal Bath / Wyndham's Theatre), Hobson's Choice (Vaudeville Theatre & UK Tour), This House (UK Tour), Martine (Finborough Theatre), The Play About My Dad (Jermyn Street Theatre), Indecent, The Grönholm

Method & *She Loves Me* (Menier Chocolate Factory), *A Christmas Carol* (Old Vic), *The Famous Five*, *Orpheus Descending* & *Insignificance* (Theatr Clwyd), *Sweet Bird of Youth* & *The House They Grew Up In* (Chichester Festival Theatre).

Television credits include: *The Seven Dials Mystery*, *Wolf Hall: The Mirror and The Light*, *The Crown*, *House of the Dragon*, *Heartstopper*, *Slow Horses*, *Renegade Nell*.

Film credits include: *Bohemian Rhapsody*, *The People We Hate at the Wedding*, *Mary Queen of Scots*, *The Secret Garden*, *Pixie*.

EVELIEN VAN CAMP
Costume Supervisor

Orange Tree Theatre credits include: *Treasure Island*, *Suite in Three Keys*, *The Circle* and *The Swell*.

Evelien has a background as assistant director, stage manager and production manager for various theatres and opera houses in Europe. After relocating to London and rediscovering her first love, costume, she has spent the last years working as a costume supervisor, designer and maker with a particular love for mid-century fashion and visual storytelling. As costume supervisor, she has worked with renowned designers such as Louie Whitemore, Anna Yates, Natasha Jenkins, Bettina John, Nate Gibson, Amy Jane Cook and Anna Reid. Venues she has worked at include the Royal Court Theatre, Park Theatre, Hampstead Theatre, Brixton House, Guildhall School of Music and Drama and Charing Cross Theatre.

She trained at the University of Antwerp in Theatre, Film and Literature studies.

CHRIS SMYTH
Wigs Supervisor & Hair Stylist

Orange Tree Theatre credits include: *Treasure Island*, *Twelfth Night*, *Suite in Three Keys*, *Testmatch*, *Uncle Vanya*, *She Stoops To Conquer* and *The Circle* (also UK tour and Theatre Royal Bath).

Theatre credits include: *The Forsyte Saga* (Park Theatre), *The Drifters Girl* (UK Tour), *Guys and Dolls* (Bridge Theatre); *Pretty Woman* (Savoy Theatre) and *9 to 5* (UK tour).

ROSIE TRICKS
Assistant Director

Rosie is currently training on the Theatre Directing MFA at Birkbeck.

Orange Tree Theatre credits as Assistant Director include: *Twelfth Night*.

As Director: *Along Came a Magpie* (Scarlet Oak Theatre), *Gus Runs Away* (Circle Theatre), *An Observation on Flirting* (Circle Theatre), *Apollo 8844* (Theatre Uncut), *Leaving Mary* (Four Steps Back).

As Assistant Director: *Animal Farm* (Rose Bruford), *Anatomy of a Suicide* (Rose Bruford), *Chitty Chitty Bang Bang* (Shinjuku Theatre Sun Mall).

MEGAN SMITH

Deputy Stage Manager

Theatre credits include: *The Circle* (UK Tour; dir. Tom Littler); *Private Lives* (West End, UK Tour, dir. Chris Luscombe); *Blithe Spirit* (West End, UK Tour, dir. Richard Eyre); *The Comedy About a Bank Robbery* (West End).

Film credits include: *Hard Truths* (dir. Mike Leigh).

Television credits include: *SAS: Who Dares Wins*, *MasterChef*, *Gangs of London*.

Events include: *The Imagination House* for Royal Caribbean Cruises.

JUDITH VOLK

Assistant Stage Manager

Orange Tree Theatre credits include: *Suite in Three Keys*, *Testmatch*.

Theatre credits include: *The Happiest Man On Earth* (Southwark Playhouse); *Room 13* (Barn Theatre); *Snakes and Ladders*, *The Watsons*, *On the Other Side of the War*, *Our Town* and *The Seagull* (Oxford School of Drama); *Elephant* (Bush Theatre); *Red Riding Hood and the Big Bad Pig* (JW3; *Fragments* (Potential Difference Theatre); *Road* and *Beryl* (Oldham Coliseum); *When The Long Trick's Over* (High Tide and New Wolsey Theatre); *Waiting for Lefty* (Two Lines Productions, online); *Amelie* (Hartshorn – Hook), and *Persuasion* (Theatre 6).

Judith also has numerous credits with Creation Theatre in Oxford, at the London Library and online, most recently *Much Ado About Nothing* at SOAP (co-pro with OVO, St Albans).

Trained at Royal Welsh College of Music and Drama.

A powerhouse of independent theatre

We are a local theatre with a global reputation.

A show at the Orange Tree is close-up magic: live, entertaining, unmissable. We're an intimate theatre with the audience wrapped around the stage. We believe in celebrating what it means to be human. We believe in putting people at the centre of the stories we tell. And we believe in the power of a writer's words, an actor's voice, and an audience's imagination to transport us to other worlds and other lives.

We punch above our weight to create world-class productions of new and contemporary drama, revitalise classics and re-discoveries, and introduce children and young people to the magic of theatre.

We are deeply rooted in our local community in South West London. We work with thousands of people aged 0 to 100 in Richmond and beyond through participatory theatre, bringing generations together to build confidence, connection, and joy. Our ground-breaking Primary Shakespeare and Shakespeare Up Close projects pack the theatre with children and ignite a spark to last a lifetime.

We're a registered charity (266128). With only 180 seats and no support from Arts Council England, we rely on the generosity of our audiences and donors to raise £650,000 a year. These funds support our outstanding work on stage and in the community and invest in the next generation of talent.

Artistic Director **Tom Littler**
Executive Director **Hanna Streeter**

orangetreetheatre.co.uk

LONDON BOROUGH OF RICHMOND UPON THAMES

THEATRE OF THE YEAR

OT TEAM

Executive
Executive Director and Joint CEO
Hanna Streeter
Artistic Director and Joint CEO
Tom Littler
Executive Assistant Reya Muller

Producing and Programming
General Manager & Producer
Sarah Murray
Carne Associate Director
Georgia Green
Literary Associate William Gregory
Associate Casting Director
Annelie Powell*
Resident Assistant Director (Birkbeck) Rosie Tricks
Trainee Production Assistant
Hetty Opayinka

Production and Technical
Production & Technical Director
Phil Bell
Company Stage Manager
Jade Gooch
Senior Production Technician
Andrew Cook
Production Technician
Priya Virdee

Community
Community Director Francesca Ellis
Community Officer Madi Mahoney
Community Associate
Jess Haygarth
Community Facilitators
Jordana Golbourn, Jess Haygarth, Madi Mahoney, Amy Tickner
Community Assistants
Heavadny Dianne C,
Sophie Kenyon, Ethan Simm

Development
Development Director
Dominique Trotter
Senior Development Officer
Katie Devey
Development Officer Rosa Stilitz

Marketing
Marketing and Sales Director
Thomas Atkinson-Joy
Marketing Officer Hannah McLelland
Interim Marketing Officer
Anna Hampton
Box Office & Sales Coordinator
Addie Uglow
CEA CAPA Intern Harry Glicklin
Graphic Designer Annie Rushton*
PR Kate Morley PR*
Box Office Team Léonie Crawford, Sophie Kenyon, Madeleine Paine

Finance, HR and operations
Deputy Executive Director Julie Weston
Finance Manager Caroline Goodwin
Finance Associate Jodie Cramphorn*
HR Consultants Bendy Ashfield and Greg Jauncey for Theatre People*

Customer Service
Front of House Manager Ben Purkiss
Duty Managers Leonie Crawford, Andrew Davidson, Tyler Deniro, Jay Hannaford, Madeleine Paine, Fenella Machin
Stewards Ailsa Auchnie, Eden Igwe, Emeka Agada, Georgina Barley, Juliet Mills, Kaitlin Reynell, Kevin Mandry, Lucy Greenhalgh, Luiza McDowell, Maire McGovern, Marie Diby, Martha Barnett, Penny Cranford, Shane Convery, Sophie Kenyon, Roanna Mcivor, Irie Page, Daisy Shaw, Tomas Caldon
Cleaner (from Miss Merry Cleaning Services) Viktor Kirov

Board Members
Feras Al-Chalabi, Anita Arora, Carolyn Backhouse, Richard Buxton, Judy Gibbons (Chair), Lesley Gregory, Marina Jones, Victoria Kent, Robert Lisney, David Marks, Corinne Meredith, India Semper-Hughes, Harriet Varley
Chair Emeritus Richard Humphreys

*Denotes Freelance or Agency

CHURCHILL IN MOSCOW

Howard Brenton

Characters

WINSTON CHURCHILL
JOSEPH STALIN
SVETLANA STALIN
VYACHESLAV MOLOTOV
SIR ARCHIBALD CLARK KERR
SALLY POWELL
OLGA DOVZHENKO

The action takes place on the 12th to the 15th of August 1942, in Moscow.

How Translation is Represented in the Play

Stalin spoke with a Georgian accent. When we understand what he is saying his English is West Country.

When there is a line that Churchill or Stalin speak directly, not through a translator, that the other cannot understand, it is shown in the script thus:

******

To the audience they are incomprehensible sounds, two gobbledegooks.

Olga Dovzhenko and Sally Powell sit very close to Stalin and to Churchill and translate to them. Most times their translations cannot be heard by the audience and are shown thus:

(*Translates.*)

At times, in the heat of the moment, the leaders jump the gun and begin to reply before their translator has finished. They become agitated in varying degrees, waiting to reply. This gives the exchanges a halting and at times strained, tense rhythm, punctuated with silences during which the leaders listen and react before they speak. It is as if the talks are happening in an enforced slow motion. As Stalin and Churchill receive the translations, they react, their body language revealing their feelings. So the play has a strong element of mime along with the dialogue.

This text went to press before the end of rehearsals and so may differ slightly from the play as performed.

Scene One: 'The Crocodile'

The Kremlin, Moscow, on the evening of the 12th of August, 1942. A room in STALIN's *apartments.*

STALIN *and* CHURCHILL *stand facing each other.*

Each has a translator. STALIN's *is* OLGA DOVZHENKO, CHURCHILL's *is* SALLY POWELL. *Both are in uniform –* OLGA *is a lieutenant in the Red Army,* SALLY *is a flight lieutenant in the RAF.*

Standing back are the Soviet Foreign Commissar, VYACHESLAV MOLOTOV, *and the British Ambassador to Moscow,* SIR ARCHIBALD CLARK KERR. *Both wear suits and have big briefcases.*

Two elaborate armchairs face each other, there is a plain hard chair beside each of them, slightly set back.

A silence. Great tension. All are still. The leaders look at each other, faces of stone. STALIN *is in a peasant's shirt, loose trousers, knee-high leather boots.* CHURCHILL *is in his trademark boiler suit.*

Then STALIN's *face creases into smiles, he takes a step forward, one foot before the other, almost leaning, and holds out his hand.*

CHURCHILL *immediately breaks too, smiles and takes* STALIN's *hand.*

They hold the handshake.

And: the play begins with STALIN *speaking to* CHURCHILL *in a Russian he cannot understand.*

STALIN. ******

CHURCHILL. Russian, dear God, sounds like a cat being sick. (*To* SALLY.) What?

SALLY (*translates to* CHURCHILL). Mr Prime Minister, welcome to the Union of Soviet Socialist Republics. It is an honour to receive you at this dark time in the lives of our great nations.

CHURCHILL. ******

STALIN. English, argh, sounds like slimy, oozy bubbles. (*To* OLGA.) Yes?

OLGA (*translates to* STALIN). He said: Mr General Secretary, I thank you from my heart for making this meeting possible, in the hope we will find the way to more speedily confound the common foe of both our peoples.

They are still holding the handshake. STALIN, *having heard the translation, releases his hand, smiles, and indicates the chair to* CHURCHILL. *He has given an impression of impeccable good manners.*

They sit.

Another unnerving silence.

NB: from now on STALIN *and* CHURCHILL*'s responses overlap the discreet translations from* OLGA *and* SALLY.

STALIN (*low, to* OLGA). The 'great' Churchill looks old. (*Loud to* CHURCHILL.) Mr Prime Minister, I understand you flew from London to Gibraltar, then on to Cairo, then to Tehran, then to us.

SALLY (*translates*).

STALIN. A journey that could fell an ox. We've met, exchanged greetings, marked this historic occasion. Why not rest now? We can begin our discussions in the morning.

SALLY (*translates*).

CHURCHILL (*low to* SALLY). The 'great' Stalin. His teeth are terrible. (*Loud to* STALIN.) I thank you for your concern. But this ox is stamping the ground, raring to go.

OLGA (*translates*).

STALIN *laughs at the 'raring to go' phrase.*

CHURCHILL. And I stopped in Cairo for a few days. To fire a general or two.

OLGA (*translates*).

STALIN *receives the translation from* OLGA *and his face creases in good humour.*

STALIN. Yes, it's always refreshing to shoot a few generals.

SALLY (*translates*).

CHURCHILL (*receives translation and laughs*). Well, we don't actually... (*To* OLGA.) Never mind.

SALLY (*low, to* CHURCHILL). He said you look old.

CHURCHILL (*not amused*). Did he.

OLGA (*low to* STALIN). He said your teeth are bad.

STALIN (*not amused*). Did he.

Another silence.

CHURCHILL. So. Mr General Secretary, I have to tell you something that you will, I fear, not want to hear. Indeed, ah in this matter, I feel I bring a lump of ice to the North Pole.

OLGA (*translates*).

STALIN *frowns.*

STALIN (*to* OLGA). Ice? Why is he talking about ice?

OLGA. I think it is a metaphor, Comrade.

STALIN. He thinks I'm made of ice?

OLGA. He's trying to say he is bringing bad news to...

She hesitates.

STALIN.... to what, more bad news? I am bad news? (*Darkening.*) The Soviet Union is bad news?

OLGA. There is an English town called Newcastle...

She continues to talk to STALIN. CHURCHILL *and* SALLY *have been watching with concern.*

CHURCHILL. What's wrong?

SALLY. I think your metaphor misfired, sir.

CHURCHILL. Why? I thought it was rather good. I'm just trying to say...

And STALIN *is speaking.*

STALIN. ****** (*Then.*) New-castle?

SALLY. He says 'Are you bringing coals to Newcastle?'

STALIN *and* CHURCHILL *stare at each other and at the same time the two translators exchange nods of recognition.*

STALIN. So what is your bad news?

SALLY (*translates*).

CHURCHILL *steels himself. As he speaks* OLGA *is translating to* STALIN.

CHURCHILL. Mr General Secretary, I have come this very long way to meet you, so our countries can understand each other. Indeed so you and I, can understand each other. To achieve that, I must speak frankly. And I invite complete frankness from you.

OLGA (*translates*).

STALIN *does not react. A silence.*

CHURCHILL *draws breath and delivers the bad news.*

OLGA *translates.*

CHURCHILL. British and American forces will not attack the Nazis in France this year. (*A beat.*) There will be no invasion across the Channel. (*A beat.*) No second front. (*A beat.*) It is the sober, deeply regretted, but realistic assessment of the British, American and Allied High Command that it will not be possible to invade, ah, until at the earliest, the spring of next year. (*A beat.*) We know this will be a hard blow and that the heroic Soviet forces are carrying a great burden...

STALIN *stands abruptly not bothering to hear the last phrases from* OLGA. CHURCHILL *stops.*

STALIN *goes to a small table and pulls open its drawer roughly. He is fiddling with something in the drawer.*

CHURCHILL *indicates 'come here' to* ARCHIBALD CLARK KERR.

Archie, what is he doing?

ARCHIE. I believe, Prime Minister, he is looking for cigarettes.

CHURCHILL. I thought he smoked a pipe.

ARCHIE *is a precise man.*

ARCHIE. He does, but he tears the cigarettes apart and stuffs the tobacco in the pipe bowl. Which is what he appears to be doing now.

CHURCHILL. It's damned hot in here.

ARCHIE. Classic Soviet central heating, I fear.

CHURCHILL. In midsummer? My trousers are sticking to my backside.

CHURCHILL *stands and walks away, pulling at the seat of his trousers.*

STALIN *is now lighting his pipe.*

MOLOTOV (*to* OLGA). I think the Prime Minister's trousers are sticking to his imperialist arse.

He smiles. OLGA *is about to laugh.*

Not a flicker!

His pipe now alight, STALIN *slams the table drawer shut and turns to face* CHURCHILL.

In response, CHURCHILL *takes a cigar case out, removes a cigar, takes out a clipper, clips the end and puts the cigar in his mouth.* ARCHIE *steps forward with a lighter.*

CHURCHILL *and* STALIN *stare at each other across the room, both smoking.*

A blackout.

Lights up.

Later. The discussions so far have been tense with suppressed bad temper. STALIN*'s pipe is out.* CHURCHILL*'s cigar is half-smoked and chewed. They have been on their feet, pacing the room.*

OLGA *and* SALLY *are working flat-out, mumbling gutturally to* STALIN *and* CHURCHILL, *who are getting impatient having to wait for translation.*

STALIN. But still I cannot understand why it is impossible to attack now.

SALLY (*translates*).

CHURCHILL. Well, as I have already told you, Hitler has twenty-five divisions in France. At the moment in England we have only six.

OLGA (*translates*).

STALIN. But those German divisions are worthless, no balls at all!

SALLY (*translates*).

CHURCHILL. Whatever their virility, our intelligence is clear – nine of Hitler's divisions are of battle-hardened, front-line veterans.

OLGA (*translates*).

STALIN. So! You cannot open a second front. And you are unwilling to land even six divisions.

SALLY (*translates*).

CHURCHILL. I know the news I bring is not good news.

OLGA (*translates*).

STALIN. Hunh!

STALIN *stuffs the unlit pipe into his mouth.*

SALLY. He grunted.

CHURCHILL (*low to* SALLY). That bit I got.

STALIN *removes the pipe.*

STALIN. I have a different view of the war. He who takes no risks never wins. Why are you so scared of the Germans? I don't understand. If you don't bloody your troops, you've no idea of their value.

SALLY (*translates*).

CHURCHILL (*low*). Oh for Christ's sake, how do I... (*Loud.*) It's geography. You are a vast country with land borders. We are an island race. Why did Hitler not invade us in 1940, when we were at our weakest, shattered, virtually on our knees? Because Hitler was afraid of the operation. It is not so easy to cross the English Channel.

OLGA (*translates*).

STALIN. No, that analogy is false. If Hitler had landed the English people would have fought him. If you land in France the people will rise and fight with you.

SALLY (*translates*).

CHURCHILL. That is true. The French population will fight with us. So it is all the more important not to expose them to the vengeance of Hitler and waste gallant lives. They will be needed when the big invasion comes. Next year.

OLGA (*translates*).

OLGA *finishes translating but* STALIN *does not reply.*

An oppressive silence.

STALIN. ******

SALLY (*translates*). Well, I cannot demand, I cannot insist, that you land in France this year. But I reject your arguments. The ice is delivered.

STALIN *nods to* MOLOTOV. *For a moment it seems that* STALIN *is about to leave the room.*

CHURCHILL. Mr General Secretary, please imagine a crocodile.

OLGA (*translates*).

STALIN (*to* OLGA). Crocodile?

OLGA. That's what he said, Comrade.

STALIN. Is he senile?

CHURCHILL. ******

OLGA. He would like a piece of paper and a pencil.

STALIN. Why?

SALLY (*translates*).

CHURCHILL. ******

OLGA. To draw a crocodile.

STALIN. Comrade Dovzhenko, are you losing something in translation here?

OLGA (*nervous*). No, Comrade.

STALIN (*shouts*). Then someone get him a fucking piece of paper!

A startled MOLOTOV *exits.*

CHURCHILL (*alarmed. Low*). What was that?

SALLY. He's getting what you want.

CHURCHILL (*low*). Hunh. My father used to shout at his butler that way.

STALIN (*to* OLGA). What did he say?

OLGA (*very uneasy*). Something about a butler.

STALIN. Butler!?

He glares at CHURCHILL. CHURCHILL *glares back.*

Do you know, Mr Prime Minister, you are the very first English aristocrat I have come face to face with.

SALLY (*translates*).

SALLY finishes translation for CHURCHILL. *A moment.*

CHURCHILL. Ah, and you, Mr General Secretary, are the very first Georgian peasant I have come face to face with.

OLGA (*translates*).

OLGA finishes translating. The two leaders continue to stare at each other, there is no good humour in the moment.

STALIN. I begin to wonder... if we can understand each other at all.

SALLY (*translates*).

SALLY finishes translating. CHURCHILL *does not reply at once.*

CHURCHILL. We must understand each other. The lives of hundreds of millions depend upon it. Ah, history holds its breath for us.

OLGA (*translates*).

STALIN, *unimpressed by the rhetoric, grunts.*

SALLY. He...

CHURCHILL. Grunted. Yes.

A moment. Then MOLOTOV *enters carrying a child's easel with rolls of paper on it and crayons.*

MOLOTOV (*to* STALIN). This may serve, Comrade, it's from the Kremlin kindergarten.

SALLY (*translates*).

STALIN. Very well, very well.

SALLY (*translates*).

CHURCHILL. You have a kindergarten in the Kremlin?

OLGA (*translates*).

STALIN (*short-tempered*). We are a Socialist country, even in war all the people's needs are met.

SALLY (*translates*).

CHURCHILL (*to* SALLY). Let that one pass.

CHURCHILL *springs to his feet. Sudden energy. He begins to draw vigorously on the easel.*

A second front, yes, but where? The situation in Europe is like...

Drawing. He finishes. A crude crocodile.

OLGA (*translates*).

Then she is translating as CHURCHILL*'s speech goes on.*

CHURCHILL. A crocodile. Its back, the French coast, heavily defended by the Nazis. Thick armour, hard to penetrate. But southern Europe, the Mediterranean, is a soft underbelly. Hitler expects invasion from England – which will come, but we can divert Hitler's attention away from the Channel – by attacking the underbelly of the beast!

OLGA (*translates*).

OLGA *finishes translating.* STALIN *shrugs, apparently unimpressed.*

CHURCHILL. Mr General Secretary, with the agreement of the Americans, I will now tell you of a major operation. But in the utmost secrecy.

A moment. Then STALIN *grins.*

STALIN. ****** *Daily Mail.*

SALLY. He says he hopes nothing about it will appear in the British press.

CHURCHILL *is momentarily put off his stride by this.* STALIN *gives a short laugh at his reaction.*

CHURCHILL. Ah. The, the operation is codenamed Torch. We will attack the Germans, landing in Morocco, Algeria, Tunisia, pushing them into Libya. And when the Nazis are cleared out of North Africa, look what is open, the crocodile's belly... Italy, the South of France. Operation Torch will be a second front. We will rip the flesh out of the croc's belly!

OLGA (*translates*).

OLGA *finishes the translation but* STALIN *is inert. A pause. Then he sits up, alert and interested.*

STALIN. When will the attack begin?

SALLY (*translates*).

CHURCHILL. Not later than October the 30th. But with President Roosevelt I am trying to push the date forward to October 7th.

OLGA (*translates*).

STALIN. October. Interesting, interesting.

SALLY (*translates*).

A pause. STALIN *thinks for a moment.*

STALIN. Hunh. (*A beat.*) But France. The French people will say why are you liberating sand dunes, not our country?

SALLY (*translates*).

CHURCHILL. I will make General de Gaulle understand.

OLGA (*translates*).

STALIN. Is de Gaulle the stubborn prick our intelligence says he is?

SALLY *hesitates*.

CHURCHILL (*to* SALLY). What?

SALLY. He was rude about the general.

CHURCHILL. Well, we agree about something.

CHURCHILL *stands. A torrent of words.*

We must not fear reality, we must be brutally frank with each other, though we be from different worlds, different cultures, for we are faced with the same disease, the terrible infection of the spirit that is Hitlerism, the very desecration of what it is to be human, for if we do not, if we cannot see the reality of the threat, if we cannot, despite the vast gulf of beliefs and ideologies between us, if we cannot make that leap and act as one, then the lights will go out, civilisation will be lost to the barbarism of the Hitlerite darkness. But if we can unite, reach out to the common humanity of our great peoples, then darkness will, in the end, be defeated, and, ah, light will once again flood the world.

OLGA (*translates*).

But she loses track during this outburst and is distressed.

Forgive me, Comrade, he spoke so fast...

STALIN. I got the spirit and I like it. The man may be a dog but he's a fighting one.

STALIN *springs out of his chair, energised.* CHURCHILL *stands in response. The two translators stand with them.*

A second front in the south, yes, I see it. I understand, that when you were in Cairo on your way here, you appointed a new commander? General Montgomery? To lead the Eighth Army?

SALLY (*translates*).

CHURCHILL (*low*). He knows about Montgomery?

SALLY. That's what he said.

CHURCHILL. Your intelligence is excellent, Mr General Secretary.

OLGA (*translates*).

STALIN (*fist held up*). If you want power, you must know what people are doing. All the time. (*Fist jerked down.*)

SALLY (*translates*).

SALLY *is a little nervous about translating this. But* CHURCHILL *laughs.*

CHURCHILL. Absolutely.

A pause. Next three lines are not translated.

STALIN (*Russian accent*). Torch.

CHURCHILL. Torch.

STALIN (*very thick accent*). Op-er-ration Torch.

A pause.

May you, with God's help, succeed.

SALLY (*translates*).

CHURCHILL *is a little startled.*

CHURCHILL (*low*). He said 'God'?

SALLY *nods.*

Yes, with His help, we shall.

OLGA (*translates*).

STALIN *offers his hand. They shake.*

Scene Two: 'Gold Taps'

Dacha No. 7. Bright light. Marble, gold.

Discovered: ARCHIE, *with a file. He is pacing, looking through it. Enter* SALLY. *She stops, looking up.*

SALLY. Goodness.

ARCHIE. Lieutenant Powell? Is something the matter?

SALLY. It's… that chandelier.

He looks up.

ARCHIE. Yes. Dangling hammers and sickles.

SALLY. Remarkable. A house like this near Moscow.

ARCHIE. Well, Dacha No. 7 is rather special.

SALLY. The marble everywhere, spotless, and the electric light. It hurts your eyes.

ARCHIE. The wall, the wire, the guard posts?

SALLY (*grimaces*). It's so...

He at once puts his fingers to his lips.

ARCHIE. I agree, it is very generous of the General Secretary to lend the Prime Minister his personal residence.

They look at each other for a moment, now highly aware of being bugged.

It is my understanding that, for the duration of these talks, the General Secretary has moved to his apartments in the Kremlin. I sense that he wishes the Prime Minister to be as comfortable as possible.

Enter CHURCHILL *in a dressing gown with a towel around his neck, slippers. He carries a "78 gramophone record in its brown sleeve.*

CHURCHILL. The bloody bath taps are solid gold! Brought this all the way with me! 'Crown Imperial'! I love a march at bedtime but there doesn't seem to be a bloody gramophone. (*Realises* SALLY *is there*.) Oh, Sally, I apologise, you find me dishabille.

SALLY (*laughs*). Not at all, Prime Minister.

She turns to go.

CHURCHILL. No no stay, I want to talk. Archie, I saw next door, in what I take to be the dining room, a vast cornucopia of liquids displayed for our, ah, possible confusion. Could you forage me a brandy?

ARCHIE. Certainly.

CHURCHILL. Do join me.

ARCHIE. I think not if you don't mind, sir, the hour... Oh very well.

CHURCHILL. You, Sally?

SALLY. Oh, a vodka, please!

CHURCHILL. With?

SALLY. Straight.

CHURCHILL. Ah. Woman after my own heart. (*Smiles, pleased.*)

ARCHIE *goes, somewhat put out.*

So. What do you make of Uncle Joe?

SALLY *looks up at the ceiling.*

Oh flobble do. Speak parrot, truth to power. Truth to power, who said that?

SALLY. I think... Socrates.

CHURCHILL. Ah.

A beat.

Yes language. Love my native tongue of course but I find it... something of a cage, delicious to rattle the bars, but... I do a kind of French... taken somewhat comically by the natives... but. Tell me, Stalin's from Georgia?

SALLY. Yes.

CHURCHILL. Speaking with a Georgian accent.

SALLY. Oh markedly. He's from the south of the Soviet Union of course, so maybe... West Country? Devon, Cornwall?

CHURCHILL. Ah. So, to Moscow ears, he's a bit of a yokel. Like an outsider? That's interesting. (*Ruminating.*) The mentality of an outsider. Against the grain. Bumpy against colleagues going the wrong way, mm, know that, all too well. Ahh.

He is looking down, at nothing. SALLY *waits, his manner concerns her – is the old man past it? Then* CHURCHILL *is all energy again.*

Bit of fun, tell me, what would I sound like in Russian?

SALLY (*hesitates*). Well… Er…

CHURCHILL. Come on!

SALLY. I'd say… old-school St Petersburg.

ARCHIE *is entering with a tray of drinks.*

CHURCHILL. You mean 'plummy'? A Russian silver spoon in my mouth? Well. I'd have been up against a wall and shot long ago! Where's the alcohol… (*He sees* ARCHIE.) Oh, Mr Ambassador, thank you so very much.

ARCHIE. A pleasure.

The tray on a small table. CHURCHILL *and* SALLY *take their drinks. They raise them to each other and drink.*

CHURCHILL. Well, a triumph.

ARCHIE. Very much so.

CHURCHILL. Sticky at first. For a moment I thought we were being shown the door.

ARCHIE. But he was very quick on the uptake about Torch.

CHURCHILL. Yes. You sense the strength of mind there. I mean this is the man who refused to abandon this city when the Nazi tanks were at the gates, what… two miles away? And let everyone know he was staying.

ARCHIE. He is a great commander.

CHURCHILL. But?

ARCHIE. Maybe we should… take the buts for granted. For now.

CHURCHILL. You mean the brutality?

ARCHIE. I… (*He points up at the ceiling.*)

CHURCHILL (*makes a dismissive wave*). That savagery will save his country. Maybe it takes a man who has killed millions to save millions.

ARCHIE (*low*). For God's sake, Winston!

CHURCHILL. Whoops. (*He laughs and drinks.*) One thing that almost hit me for six. When he said 'God'.

A pause. ARCHIE *and* SALLY *are reluctant to engage in this.*

ARCHIE. It could have been... well, a form of flattery. Knowing we're Church of England.

CHURCHILL. I don't think the Church of England has ever been much on Stalin's mind.

SALLY. I think he meant it.

CHURCHILL. This is the man who had a hundred thousand priests shot in one go! A militant, dyed-in-the-wool, hard-core, iron-clad Marxist atheist!

SALLY. He did train to be a priest himself.

CHURCHILL. Isn't that story propaganda?

ARCHIE. No it's probably true. He was sent to a seminary in Tbilisi when he was fourteen.

CHURCHILL. Ha! And found Marx, not God.

ARCHIE. Absolutely.

CHURCHILL. So why's he invoking the will of the Almighty?

SALLY. He probably meant 'fate' more than anything. It's deep in the Russian soul. Life and fate, they are the same thing.

CHURCHILL. But it's a clue, an insight, an opening, to burrow into the heart of the man.

ARCHIE. Do we want to journey into Stalin's heart?

CHURCHILL. A terrifying prospect, yes. But, but. Maybe not all is as it seems with Uncle Joe. Maybe I can come to understand him. Mm.

He is lost in thought for a moment, clutching the glass of brandy to his chest. Then he snaps out of it, finishes his drink and puts the glass down on the tray.

Well, it may not be very Church of Englandy of me to say this, even a touch Marxy, but I believe, in these few days, we have our fate in our own hands. And I nigh dare not say it, because it is true... the fate of millions. But we have made a champion start! And now we should go to bed! Be fresh and bushy-tailed for the morning!

ARCHIE. Yes indeed, Prime Minister, goodnight.

SALLY. Goodnight, sir.

They exit.

CHURCHILL *alone. He stands still. Then he moves to the drinks and pours himself another glass. He picks it up. Looks at it and then exits, shambling a little.*

The stage is empty for a while.

Then a FIGURE, *lean, fit, dressed in black, enters quickly carrying a magnificently horned, gold-coloured gramophone. He places it in the middle of the stage and exits.*

Again for a while nothing happens. We look at the gramophone.

A blackout.

In the blackout, the climax of William Walton's 'Crown Imperial' plays. It stops and...

Birdsong.

Lights up slowly into a glorious, morning light streaming in.

Enter ARCHIE, *briskly. He is in a suit, carrying a briefcase. He stops in his tracks when he sees the gramophone.*

CHURCHILL *enters from the garden. He is in slacks and shirtsleeves, no tie, mules on his feet. He carries a cup of coffee.*

CHURCHILL. Don't know if this has anything to do with coffee, but their chicory, if that what it be, is excellent. Good morning, Archie.

ARCHIE. Good morning, Prime Minister. (*Re: the gramophone.*) This...

CHURCHILL. I know. Appeared magically and fully functional. I've had 'Crown Imperial' on already.

ARCHIE. Oh that was you, thought I heard music... around four last night...

CHURCHILL. Couldn't sleep. The excitement! God, Archie, today we may actually have an agreement with the Soviets.

ARCHIE. The signs in the entrails do look good. Molotov is here to discuss the timetable.

CHURCHILL. Then in, in, march him in!

ARCHIE. One thing. Molotov has excellent English, but will speak Russian.

CHURCHILL. Bloody-minded!

ARCHIE. And you address him as Commissar, not as Foreign Secretary.

CHURCHILL. I'll address him as a time-serving Bolshie little shit!

ARCHIE. We are on a knife edge. The little things matter.

CHURCHILL. They do indeed. Like no plug in the bath. (*Points to the ceiling.*) Oops! Now there will be.

ARCHIE. I'll... Yes.

ARCHIE *exits*.

Nimbly CHURCHILL *makes for the drinks table and pours a shot of brandy into his coffee cup.*

ARCHIE *enters with* MOLOTOV, OLGA *and* SALLY. OLGA *carries a briefcase. She sets it down beside her foot.*

MOLOTOV. ******, Prime Minister.

SALLY. Good morning, Prime Minister.

CHURCHILL. ******, Commissar.

OLGA. Good morning, Commisar.

From here the translators speak quietly, just behind CHURCHILL *and* MOLOTOV. *Stiffness.*

MOLOTOV. I hope you slept well.

SALLY (*translates*).

CHURCHILL. Well, but very little. There is much to think about.

OLGA (*translates*).

MOLOTOV. There is indeed.

SALLY (*translates*).

CHURCHILL. I understand you wish to discuss the, ah, timetable.

OLGA (*translates*).

MOLOTOV. Comrade Stalin has meetings during the day with the Soviet Army High Command, I'm sure you understand why.

SALLY (*translates*).

CHURCHILL. Indeed yes, I hope the news from the front is good.

OLGA (*translates*).

MOLOTOV. You called for frankness last night. I have to tell you the news is not good. Hitler's Sixth Army continues its advance in the south. There is a serious threat to the city of Stalingrad.

SALLY (*translates*).

CHURCHILL. I appreciate the information. My thoughts and prayers are with the heroic Soviet forces.

OLGA (*translates*).

MOLOTOV *finds this remark distasteful but keeps his council.*

MOLOTOV. Would it be convenient to meet late evening?

SALLY (*translates*).

CHURCHILL. Perfect. Perhaps at ten o'clock?

OLGA (*translates*).

MOLOTOV. If it is not too difficult, could it be eleven?

SALLY (*translates*).

CHURCHILL. Eleven is excellent. Something of a night bird myself.

OLGA (*translates*).

CHURCHILL (*over* OLGA). Been known to roar through the small hours at the London Ritz till the dawn, no, Archie?

ARCHIE (*a terrible memory*). Yes indeed, sir.

This knocks OLGA *from her rhythm. But then* CHURCHILL *is speaking again and she picks up.*

CHURCHILL. Commissar. I trust that the General Secretary is not going to treat us roughly. To do so would be a very serious mistake.

OLGA (*translates*).

A pause, MOLOTOV *taking some time to consider this. Then his face creases into a smile.*

MOLOTOV. No no, be assured. We are all enemies of fascism. We will be friends. Comrade Stalin is a very wise man, he understands what is at stake. He will make the evening very agreeable. I will tell him what you have said. Thank you, Prime Minister.

SALLY (*translates*).

CHURCHILL. Thank you, Commissar.

They shake hands.

OLGA *makes a brief bow.* SALLY *responds.* OLGA *and* MOLOTOV *exit.*

CHURCHILL *is suddenly furious.*

Did Molotov actually say he was an enemy of fascism?

SALLY. Well, yes.

CHURCHILL. The man who negotiated peace with Hitler? Left us all alone in 1940?

ARCHIE. I don't think...

CHURCHILL.... Hobnobbed with Goering, Goebbels and all the gang? And now the man who put his tongue up Adolf's arse has the cheek to say he is anti-fascist?

ARCHIE (*terrified of the bugging*). Winston, shut up!

A silence.

Then CHURCHILL*'s mood switches. He grins.*

CHURCHILL (*shouts up at the ceiling*). My enemy's enemy is my friend! (*To* SALLY *and* ARCHIE.) Funny thing, history, topsy-turvy, up and down and inside out, all around the roundabout. Yes. But we're in it, on it, riding it, so – hold on for dear life!!

Scene Three: 'The Devil's Egg'

Kremlin. The room set up for the conference – armchairs.

STALIN *is sitting in his chair, dead still, legs and arms splayed, staring at nothing.*

Enter SVETLANA STALIN, *aged sixteen. She wears a blue-spotted, short-sleeved summer frock.*

She stands a distance away, uncertain.

STALIN *comes to and sees her.*

STALIN. Ah! My little hostess.

SVETLANA. Little Papa…

STALIN. You should be in bed, my dear.

SVETLANA. It's so noisy, doors keep banging, people rushing about. Has the front moved near to us again?

STALIN. No it's not the Germans. It's the British.

SVETLANA. The British have attacked?

STALIN (*laughs*). In a way they're trying to! Come, join Little Papa.

He pulls the translator's chair round. She sits on it.

Your dress is very pretty.

SVETLANA. I'm just trying things on. There's the party in the House of Government on Sunday, with the Andropovs.

STALIN. That's nice. But that one's not for a party, the sleeves are too short.

SVETLANA. Oh don't be a grump.

STALIN. Grump? Ha!… (*A beat.*) Your mother loved blue dresses.

SVETLANA. I remember.

STALIN. I don't think you do.

SVETLANA. In the summer, at…

STALIN. No no, you were only six.

SVETLANA. Yes but everything before I was six is… bright memory.

STALIN. 'Bright memory'! Pushkin?

SVETLANA (*nods*). 'In silence…'

STALIN *and* SVETLANA (*quoting*). 'In silence bright memory unfurls her scroll…'

STALIN. Yes, yes. Morbid stuff. (*He takes her hand, tenderly.*) Memory is worthless. Even dangerous. It stops us doing what we have to.

SVETLANA. Can't I wear blue, like Mama?

STALIN. Of course you can, sweetheart. But with long sleeves.

SVETLANA. No! I'm going to the Andropovs' party and I'm wearing this dress! I can do anything I like, I'm a Stalin too!

STALIN. No you are not! Listen, listen to me, little one. You're not Stalin. And I'm not Stalin. Stalin is Soviet power. Stalin is what is in the newspapers and the portraits, not you, no, not even me!

SVETLANA. Then... who are we?

STALIN. In ourselves? People of no importance.

She tries to pull her hand away.

(*Holding on to her hand.*) But, here, for now, we can be Little Papa and Little Hostess...

She will not give him her hand.

I know it's hard, Svetlana. But we have no choice. We are what we are, where we are.

Takes her hand suddenly. She does not resist.

Do you want to meet Winston Churchill?

SVETLANA. *The* Winston Churchill? The great imperialist?

STALIN. That's the one.

SVETLANA. He's in Moscow?

STALIN. Oh yes. That's a very big secret, Svetlana.

SVETLANA. But... how did he get here?

STALIN. The Devil flew him, in a giant egg.

SVETLANA. Oh the Devil in the story, turned himself into a black goose...

STALIN. And laid an evil egg in the henhouse...

SVETLANA. And the egg cracked open and a fox broke out and ate all the hens! I love the fairy tales, but now I'm older I think, 'Why are they so violent?'

STALIN. Tell me one great book that is not violent.

She thinks.

SVETLANA. Goncharov's *Oblomov*?

STALIN *laughs*.

STALIN. The story of a man who refuses to get out of bed?

SVETLANA. He stays in bed and does no harm.

STALIN. But look at it like this, isn't Oblomov's sloth, an act of violence? He neglects his friends, his family, everything around him falls into chaos because he does nothing. Doing nothing is a form of extreme brutality.

SVETLANA. It's just a funny book.

STALIN. Oh it's funny enough.

SVETLANA. So... Winston Churchill...

STALIN. Has come out of his egg in the middle of Moscow, yes. I may have to have a serious talk to him, in private. I know I call you it for fun, and because I love you so very much... but would you be hostess, for your father and Winston Churchill?

SVETLANA. Yes. Yes, what would you want to eat?

STALIN. What do you suggest?

SVETLANA. Suckling pig!

STALIN (*laughs*). Hoo-hoo!

SVETLANA. Cooked over coals, on a spit, with an apple in its mouth?

STALIN. And a black egg up its backside!

SVETLANA. Yes!

STALIN. Because you're thinking...

SVETLANA. He's a British aristo...

STALIN. A pig!

SVETLANA. A pig!

STALIN *and* SVETLANA. So let him eat one!

They laugh.

SVETLANA. And I know it's your favourite too.

Laughter goes.

STALIN. You must go away now.

SVETLANA. Yes, Father.

STALIN. If we do have Churchill to dinner, you can wear those sleeves.

She looks at him. There is almost a moment when it seems she is going to curtsy. She turns and exits.

STALIN *recites from memory.*

Noisy day no more assaults the ears
As, slowly on the silent city,
Night's shadow falls and men, worn out by work,
Are paid their wages in deep sleep.
But not I: wide awake, I find no peace
Within the silent, weary hours,
As through the listless night the serpents of remorse
Pierce me with their vicious fangs.
Obsessed with seething dreams, the soul
Cannot bear or cure the pain.
In silence bright memory unfurls her scroll
Before me, and, alone, I must endure
The record of the bitter years in deep regret.

He is still for a while. Then laughter begins to well up in him.

Alexander, Alexander, Sasha, Sasha Pushkin! Russia's greatest? No. Just a spewer-out of pretty phrases. The tinkling of words as music, that's all. If you'd have been alive now, dearly beloved Sasha Sasha, I'd have to bang you up for bourgeois formalism! 'Regret'? What is there to regret? A little piddle of piss in the trouser leg? That you can regret. The rest is... (*A moment, thinks.*) The rest is... (*A beat.*) With Hamlet. Silence. (*Laughs.*) Poetry? Thank the fuck I gave up trying to write the stuff years ago! (*Laughs, then he is silent again.*) Pretty words. Pretty sleeves.

Enter MOLOTOV.

MOLOTOV. Churchill's car is inside the gates.

STALIN. Good. Anything from Timoshenko?

MOLOTOV. Not overnight.

STALIN. The moment he reports, I am to be told. Even if I'm with the British.

MOLOTOV. Of course. The transcripts from the tapes at the dacha are in.

STALIN. Are they fun?

MOLOTOV. Churchill played military music at four in the morning.

STALIN. Ha! What? To gee himself up? Well, we will see. Put them on my desk. (*A moment then he decides.*) I am going to telegraph new orders to Timoshenko.

MOLOTOV. Communications may be down, he is moving his HQ.

STALIN. I should hope the fuck he is.

MOLOTOV. What will your orders be?

STALIN. To cooperate with NKVD barrier units.

MOLOTOV. You are deploying the barrier units?

STALIN. A mile behind the front line. All deserters to be shot on sight.

MOLOTOV. Excellent.

STALIN. Not excellent, Slava. Just necessary. A terrible fight is coming in the south. Keep the British sweet.

STALIN exits quickly. MOLOTOV *looks around, moves the hard chair next to* STALIN*'s armchair back to its position then exits.*

Empty stage for a while.

Enter MOLOTOV *with* CHURCHILL, SALLY *and* ARCHIE.

MOLOTOV. ******

SALLY. The General Secretary is communicating with the Commander of the Red Army on the river Volga. He apologises and will be with you directly.

CHURCHILL. ******

OLGA. No apology necessary, on the contrary. I, eh, hope the news from the front is good.

MOLOTOV. ******

SALLY. The heroic struggle of the Red Army continues.

CHURCHILL. Ah. Excellent.

And MOLOTOV *and* OLGA *exit quickly.*

ARCHIE. I fear they're letting us sweat a little.

CHURCHILL. I fear they're losing a war. (*A beat.*) Listen! Is the water actually boiling in the radiators?

ARCHIE. I...

Enter STALIN *and* OLGA. *A little after them,* MOLOTOV *re-enters, discreetly.*

STALIN, *smiling, shakes hands with* CHURCHILL. *As the pleasantries unfold an unease settles over the occasion.*

STALIN. I hope you slept well, Mr Prime Minister.

SALLY (*translates*).

CHURCHILL. Extremely well, Mr General Secretary.

OLGA (*translates*).

STALIN. If you lack anything, please let me know.

SALLY (*translates*).

CHURCHILL. Everything I could possibly need you have provided, including an excellent brandy.

OLGA (*translates*).

STALIN. I hope we will have a real drink together, at the end of our little talk tonight.

SALLY (*translates*).

CHURCHILL. A real Russian drink will be excellent. In the ways of vodka, I will be guided.

OLGA (*translates*).

STALIN. I meant the wines from where I was born, Georgia.

SALLY (*translates*).

CHURCHILL. I look forward to a journey into an alcoholic terra incognito.

CHURCHILL grins, hoping the phrase has gone down well. It has not.

They sit.

Unsmiling, STALIN *sits upright in the chair.*

A silence.

STALIN. Mr Prime Minister. Why are you shit-scared of the Germans?

ARCHIE. Oh God no.

SALLY. Oh horrible little man.

CHURCHILL *looks at her.*

(*Hesitates then translates.*)

CHURCHILL (*low*). He said I'm frightened of the Germans?

SALLY. Actually, he used a stronger term.

CHURCHILL. What 'term'?

SALLY *whispers to him.*

Sally, you must translate exactly.

SALLY. Yes, sir, I'm sorry.

CHURCHILL. Don't be. This is the clash of two worlds. (*He turns to* STALIN.) I am not aware of being brown-trousered about anyone, Mr General Secretary.

OLGA (*translates*).

STALIN (*low; to* OLGA). Brown-what?

OLGA. He says he does not soil himself.

STALIN (*low*). No? Let's see what we can do. (*To* CHURCHILL.) Why have you stopped sending us weapons by convoy through the Arctic Ocean?

SALLY (*translates*).

CHURCHILL. I did apologise by telegram. The sea route to Archangel is most hazardous. German U-boats control it. Our last convoy, PQ17, was all but wholly destroyed. Twenty-three ships were sunk. Hundreds of tanks, hundreds of aircraft, thousands of vehicles, an entire fleet, now at the bottom of the Arctic Ocean. It was an unmitigated disaster. This is what I mean when I say we must be frank with each other, face reality. The brutal truth is we cannot afford to lose more ships.

OLGA (*translates*).

STALIN (*to* OLGA). Brutal truths? The man babbles of brutal truths?

OLGA. Yes, Comrade…

STALIN (*to* CHURCHILL). I too have a brutal truth! We have a desperate need for more weapons!

SALLY (*translates*).

CHURCHILL. The British Navy is dangerously depleted. We cannot risk more convoys until we have more ships from America.

OLGA (*translates*).

STALIN. America, America, why is Britain forever chewing on America's tits?

SALLY *hesitates*.

CHURCHILL (*low to her*). Never mind.

STALIN. This is the first time in history the British Navy has run away from a fight!

Again SALLY *is hesitant.*

CHURCHILL (*low*). Tell me.

SALLY (*translates*).

CHURCHILL. That is a wholly unjustified slur.

OLGA (*translates*).

STALIN. It is the truth. You will not attack.

SALLY (*translates*).

CHURCHILL. We are attacking, in North Africa… with Operation Torch…

OLGA (*translates*).

STALIN (*over* OLGA*'s translation*). You've got six divisions in England sat on their arses. I cannot understand why you do not use them.

SALLY (*translates*).

CHURCHILL. I had hoped I'd been understood. When, ah, the German forces in North Africa have been defeated, we will invade Europe from the south, the soft belly of the crocodile.

SALLY (*translates*).

SCENE THREE   35

STALIN (*scoffs*). 'Soft', 'soft'. You are shit-scared of doing the hard job in northern France!

SALLY *is hating this.*

SALLY (*translates*).

CHURCHILL *controls himself with difficulty. A beat.*

CHURCHILL. Again. I repeat what was explained yesterday. We will attack in France, but we cannot until next year.

OLGA *is also hating the heat of the exchanges.*

OLGA (*translates*).

STALIN (*over his translator*). If the British Army had fought the Germans as much as the Red Army has, they wouldn't be so scared. So, as you say, 'brown-trousered'.

SALLY (*translates*).

CHURCHILL (*addressing* OLGA *directly*). Madam translator, please explain very clearly that I forgive these remarks on account of the bravery of the Russian troops.

OLGA (*translates*).

STALIN (*ignoring* OLGA). Yes! And the Red Army is, at this very moment, fighting all alone in Europe. While you play sand pits in North Africa and cringe behind your English white cliffs.

SALLY (*translates*).

STALIN (*shouting, straight at* CHURCHILL). ******!

CHURCHILL *is dumbfounded.*

SALLY. He said... said... 'What are you, cowards?'

CHURCHILL, *seething, still manages to control himself.*

MOLOTOV. Joseph...

STALIN. Just cracking the Devil's egg.

CHURCHILL (*low to* SALLY). And what the hell was that?

SALLY. Something about an egg...

CHURCHILL. Egg? Egg? I'm not taking this. (*To* STALIN.) May I remind the General Secretary, that for two years, of great peril, Britain was entirely alone in Europe, fighting the Nazis. Alone, because you had made a pact with Hitler's gang. (*Pointing at* MOLOTOV.) The man standing there signed it. Where was he? Quaffing champagne with Hermann Goering in his hunting lodge! We stood firm in the darkest days, you did not. So do not doubt our British resolve.

OLGA (*translates*).

STALIN *does not seem to be listening.* OLGA *finishes.*

A silence.

Then, abruptly, STALIN *stands.*

STALIN. Tomorrow there is a banquet. It is in your honour.

He exits quickly before SALLY *finishes translating.*

SALLY (*translates*).

CHURCHILL *stands. He stares at* MOLOTOV *who, with a ghost of a short bow, turns and leaves.*

CHURCHILL. Archie. Car. Now.

He exits quickly, followed by ARCHIE.

SALLY *and* OLGA *are left on the stage, looking at each other. They speak in English.*

SALLY. A bit hairy there.

OLGA. Hairy?

SALLY. Difficult.

OLGA *shrugs. But they want to talk. A beat.*

OLGA. 'Alcoholic terra incognito.' Is that a British upper-class saying?

SALLY. No, Mr Churchill made it up.

OLGA. Of interest though. 'Unknown land.'

SALLY. He was probably thinking of Scott of the Antarctic.

OLGA. Who?

SALLY. A British Explorer.

OLGA. Ah. This is the imperialist mentality.

SALLY. Absolutely.

A beat.

The egg thing. What was that about?

OLGA. It's an old Georgian fairy tale. Comrade Stalin is fond of it.

SALLY. The peasant mentality.

OLGA. Absolutely.

Then they smile at each other.

SALLY. Your uniform, you're Red Army?

OLGA. Yes. You are Royal Air Force?

SALLY. I'm a flight lieutenant, seconded from Fighter Command.

OLGA. Lieutenant is my rank too. Seconded from the Fifth Tank Destroyer Division. I should be fighting.

SALLY. Oh I think we are, don't you?

A beat.

I must...

OLGA. I too.

They exit.

A pause.

SVETLANA *wanders on, reading from* David Copperfield *Chapter XI. She stops.*

SVETLANA. 'I remember two pudding shops, between which I was divided, according to my finances. One was in a court close to St Martin's Church – at the back of the church – which is now removed altogether. The pudding at that shop was made of currants, and was rather a special pudding, but was dear, twopennyworth being larger than a pennyworth of more ordinary pudding. A good shop for the latter was in the Strand – somewhere in that part which has been rebuilt since. It was a stout pale pudding, heavy and flabby, and with great flat raisins in it, stuck in whole at wide distances apart. It came up hot at about my time every day, and many a day did I dine off it.'

She hears something. She closes the book and runs off.

A blackout.

Scene Four: 'Speaking to Trees'

The garden of Dacha No. 7. Night.

Bright lights throw hard shadows of trees across the stage.

CHURCHILL (*off*). Archie! Garden!

  CHURCHILL *enters fast,* ARCHIE *follows.*

  So.

ARCHIE. So.

CHURCHILL. We were doing so well. Then suddenly that!

ARCHIE. It is a setback.

CHURCHILL. Setback?! He insulted the British fighting man!

ARCHIE. Maybe it's just a technique.

CHURCHILL. Technique?!

ARCHIE. A diplomatic ploy.

CHURCHILL. I see no diplomacy. He accused us of cowardice! To my face! If the translation was right.

ARCHIE. Spot-on, I'm afraid.

CHURCHILL. He is an evil and dreadful man!

ARCHIE (*looking around nervously*). I think we can take that as a given...

CHURCHILL. How can you deal with evil? When promises are rat poison put down to kill truth? When words become lies that eat, like acid into... (*Improvising*.) into the very fabric of understanding? Then trust is impossible, and no one can agree what the world is like, let alone how to... act! Govern! Win a war! The foul breath of the Russian bear, ha! I smelt it on that man, through the vile teeth, the vile tobacco.

ARCHIE. Prime Minister, can I remind you that even the garden...

CHURCHILL. What, he's bugged the trees too? So what are we standing in? A prison yard? Yes, in a maze of prisons... (*Shouting at the trees*.) Russia! You are a stinking gaol! And the stench comes from your gaoler, Joseph Stalin, who is a murderer and a thug! Thug, thug, who...

He is suddenly breathless, drained of energy. He staggers a little.

ARCHIE. Prime Minister...

CHURCHILL. Long day, long day.

ARCHIE. Perhaps we should sleep on it.

CHURCHILL. No, no, can't let this go.

ARCHIE. We must not make a rash decision.

CHURCHILL. Oh it's made! It made itself! (*A beat*.) The talks have failed. We're leaving.

ARCHIE. That would be...

CHURCHILL. The land of the comrades? I sense not a jot of comradeship here. We go! First light!

ARCHIE. I think you should consider...

CHURCHILL. I have considered! Stalin and his gang are implacable foes. I sent troops to stop their revolution in 1917, but not enough of 'em! (*At the trees*.) We should have sent the whole bloody British Army!

ARCHIE. The British Army was fighting the Germans on the Somme at the time. Are you going to calm down?

CHURCHILL. I am calm!

ARCHIE. We must be rational.

CHURCHILL. I am rational! These negotiations are pointless. We are packing up, back on the plane, first thing in the morning.

ARCHIE. Winston, listen to me. I've known you many years, and I have seen you... (*Hesitates*.)

CHURCHILL. Seen me what?

ARCHIE. Make some disastrous mistakes.

CHURCHILL. Hunh! Can't think what.

ARCHIE. Yes you can. And to walk out on Stalin now would be... worse than Gallipoli. Worse than Norway. So, I have to say this, pull yourself together.

CHURCHILL. Ha! Comb my hair, pull my trousers up. Are you nannying me, Mr Ambassador?

ARCHIE. Absolutely, Prime Minister.

CHURCHILL. In Moscow, so far in time and space from our nannies.

CHURCHILL *laughs, then is touched by depression. Hunches. A beat then he revs up again.*

We reached good ground last night. He was quick to understand Operation Torch. Brute he may be, but he is not stupid! I ask myself why this sudden change?

ARCHIE. He agrees, then he hardens up. He did it with the Foreign Secretary last Christmas.

CHURCHILL. Yes but Anthony's a softie at heart, Joe Stalin sniffed the marshmallow within. I am not soft.

ARCHIE. But you are a bull at a gate. I feel I must be frank.

CHURCHILL. Frankness! Ha, that's what I was trying to achieve with him! The result? Lies, ploys, insults…

ARCHIE. There is a massive clash of civilisations here. You are an aristocrat, the heir of mighty houses and estates, dukedoms are in your blood, you are at ease with wealth and privilege.

CHURCHILL. Oh guff, guff…

ARCHIE. No, you have to understand. The Bolsheviks see themselves as coming out of nothing, generations of brutal oppression, ignorance, poverty. What are they at ease with? Only the struggle for survival. You and he are from violently different worlds, misunderstandings can be great, tempers be lost. On both sides.

CHURCHILL. You're right. (*A beat.*) More right than you realise. The divide is too great. We will never understand each other. If I stay it will get worse, I will really lose my temper! (*To the trees.*) Kick the Russian bear in the balls! (*Turning away.*) We leave. Wake the plane crew, the fuel must be checked.

ARCHIE. Allow me to ask one thing, one thing!

A beat.

CHURCHILL. Very well. Go.

ARCHIE. Why did you come to Moscow in the first place?

CHURCHILL. To hasten the end of this terrible war.

ARCHIE. Of course, but that's a quote for newspapers. Not the real reason, is it.

He looks up at the trees and decides to go on regardless.

You came because, in London, you and your government have a fear. A terrible fear.

Now even CHURCHILL *is aware of the trees.*

You are here because of it.

CHURCHILL *looks at him.*

And has it occurred to you that they have exactly the same fear about us?

CHURCHILL (*explodes*). Britain and its Empire will never make peace with Hitler! Ever! We will go to our graves, fighting.

ARCHIE (*low*). But will they?

A long silence.

CHURCHILL. Damn you, Archie. (*Ruminates.*) This banquet with the peasants.

ARCHIE. Yes.

CHURCHILL. What will happen at it?

ARCHIE. All of Stalin's inner circle will be there. Beria, with high-ranking NKVD, the entire Politburo, probably not with wives, and members of the Red Army staff.

CHURCHILL. And there will be drinks.

ARCHIE. 'Drinks' is something of an understatement. Toast on toast, more and more raucous. There will be massive good cheer all round, but be careful. Stalin holds back. He likes everyone round him to get absolutely sloshed, so the indiscretions can begin. He drinks seriously, later.

CHURCHILL. Later?

ARCHIE. Moscow is a city that works by night. You can't get hold of anyone in the day, the ministries are silent, no phone calls, locked gates. But come nightfall, the lights go on. Stalin dines at eleven and the business of government begins, messengers on motorcycles fan out from the Kremlin, the system speeds up, whirring around ever faster, until dawn. And, exhausted, people collapse into their beds.

CHURCHILL. And Stalin?

ARCHIE. They say he never sleeps. But they always say that about dictators.

CHURCHILL. It's said about me.

ARCHIE. Well, you really don't. Except after lunch...

CHURCHILL. True, dear nanny. (*Pause*.) Very well. I'll stay for the banquet. But any more insults and... I will make a scene. A mighty, turbulentual, diplomatic Krakatoa of a scene!

ARCHIE. No doubt.

CHURCHILL. Then I leave.

CHURCHILL walks away and exits.

For a moment ARCHIE *stands in the garden, his hand held to his face. Then he turns to leave.*

A blackout.

Between the scenes: SVETLANA *reading from* David Copperfield *Chapter XVIII.*

SVETLANA. 'Miss Shepherd is a boarder at the Misses Nettingalls' establishment. I adore Miss Shepherd. She is a little girl, in a spencer, with a round face and curly flaxen hair. The Misses Nettingalls' young ladies come to the Cathedral too. I cannot look upon my book, for I must look upon Miss Shepherd. When the choristers chant, I hear Miss Shepherd. In the service I mentally insert Miss Shepherd's name – I put her in among the Royal Family. At home, in my own room, I am sometimes moved to cry out, "Oh Miss Shepherd!" in a transport of love.

For sometime I was doubtful of Miss Shepherd's feelings, but at length, Fate being propitious, we meet at the dancing school. I have Miss Shepherd for my partner. I touch Miss Shepherd's glove, and feel a thrill go up the right arm of my jacket, and come out at my hair.'

She laughs and wanders away, still reading.

Scene Five: 'Unfreeze the Tundra'

Kremlin urinal. Offstage the sounds of ragged singing – a Russian song.

ARCHIE *staggers on, much the worse for wear. He disappears into a stall. Sounds of vomiting. A loo flushes.*

Enter MOLOTOV, *unsteady but not as bad as* ARCHIE. *He approaches a urinal. He uses it and calls out.*

MOLOTOV. Mr Ambassador? Speak English?

ARCHIE (*off*). Ahhh!

MOLOTOV. The Romans had vomitoriums, didn't they. It was a matter of honour to throw up at least once during a meal.

ARCHIE (*off*). Oooh.

MOLOTOV *finishes and goes to wash his hands. He looks at himself in a mirror, pulling his lower lids down to inspect his eyes.*

MOLOTOV. No red lines in the white, yet. Barely at stage two.

ARCHIE *staggers out of the stall.*

ARCHIE. What are they toasting in there now?

MOLOTOV. They've moved on from their wives and are on to their dogs.

ARCHIE. They are toasting... pets?

MOLOTOV. Your Prime Minister raised a glass to a dog called Jock.

ARCHIE. Cat.

MOLOTOV. What?

ARCHIE. Jock is Churchill's cat.

MOLOTOV. No the toast was called for dogs. It's an insult to make it for a cat!

ARCHIE. Un... unintentional.

MOLOTOV. No, an insult.

MOLOTOV's stance is aggressive. A pause.

ARCHIE. It's not going very well in there, is it.

MOLOTOV. It is like... tundral.

ARCHIE. Ah, of the Siberian earth, the tundra, deeply frozen. Deep frozen earth is right. I thought the vodka was meant to unfreeze things but it seems to be having the opp... reverse effect...

MOLOTOV. Yes that's why you and I...

But ARCHIE *is on an expansive roll.*

ARCHIE. ...I mean, I love this posting, I love the literature, the great history, the people, the music, oh the music, Tych, Muss – Muss – orsky, Shostakovich but I hate, hate... the drink.

MOLOTOV. Have you met Dmitri Shostakovich?

ARCHIE. Would *love* to.

MOLOTOV. He likes a tipple.

ARCHIE, *with a gesture of exaggerated despair.*

ARCHIE. Why, why is alcohol washing through you all?

MOLOTOV. It's a sea we swim in.

ARCHIE. But why?

MOLOTOV. To see if we don't drown. (*He laughs.*)

ARCHIE. Drown, why should you...

MOLOTOV. Let me put it like this. Lenin nearly had me shot.

ARCHIE. He was a piss artist too?

MOLOTOV. No no. Vladimir Ilyich didn't drink.

ARCHIE (*looking around him, a stagger*). The founding father of this... this... this nightmare didn't drink?

MOLOTOV. Mr Ambassador, forgive me, I need your attention! But first I suggest you have another puke.

ARCHIE. Most... excellent idea.

He crashes back into the stall. MOLOTOV *looks at himself in the mirror again. As if splashing water on his face which he then covers with his hands. After a while he removes them and looks at himself.*

MOLOTOV. It's still there. The certainty of danger. Vladimir Ilyich! A hundred and one days into the Revolution in 1917, I remember you dancing down the corridor of Party Headquarters. What's happened, I asked? Lenin said 'We've lasted one day more than the Paris Commune! We're still alive!' Yes. Any moment, we thought, we will be dead. And still, any moment, we are dead. (*A beat.*) Now, do this! Do this! Get through the night. See the dawn in, still in the job and not shot in the back of the neck. So. Save your country. Save the Revolution.

A flushing. ARCHIE *comes out of the stall.*

ARCHIE. Nothing. I think I... I have stabilised. Momentarily.

MOLOTOV. Unlike the situation.

ARCHIE. Indeed. I think I said something about Russians and alcohol just now, I do apologise, this is something of a night, of, I fear...

MOLOTOV (*interrupting*). Churchill must not leave in the morning.

A beat.

ARCHIE. How do you know he...

MOLOTOV, *an irritated gesture.*

He has made up his mind.

MOLOTOV. It's down to you to unmake it.

ARCHIE. I have tried.

MOLOTOV. The Germans are very near Stalingrad.

A touch of fear.

ARCHIE. How near?

MOLOTOV. Near.

ARCHIE. Are you trying to tell me that the Germans have, actually, taken Stalingrad?

MOLOTOV. They are near.

ARCHIE. This… this is the problem! It is gut-tearingly difficult to believe any information coming out of Moscow.

MOLOTOV (*scoffs*). Or out of London. Churchill's rubbish about Operation Torch.

ARCHIE. I cata– catgog assure you, Operation Torch is about to happen.

MOLOTOV. So is the fall of Stalingrad. Unless we spill a river of blood to defend it.

ARCHIE. 'Unless'?

MOLOTOV *is stony-faced*.

You… are you… hint–… saying you may stop fighting? That Russia is thinking of making peace with Hitler?

MOLOTOV. Churchill is!

ARCHIE. Absolutely not!

MOLOTOV. Absolutely yes! Isn't that what's behind this Churchill charade, this big barrage balloon blow-up act? Pretending to lose his temper so he can walk out of the talks, go back to London and tell your War Cabinet the Soviet Union would not agree, and that you must approach Berlin? Make peace with Hitler, then turn on us? Destroy the Soviet Union? Join with fascist Germany to wipe Socialism off the face of the earth?

ARCHIE. No. No, no! That is – paranoid.

MOLOTOV. Paranoia is a political tool. I find it highly effective.

ARCHIE. He did lose his temper. Genuinely. Britain will never stop fighting for our democracy.

MOLOTOV. And for your Empire.

ARCHIE. Of course! Never, ever stop.

MOLOTOV. If Stalingrad falls, the Soviet Union will be defeated. Then the Germans will turn their full force on Britain. And they'll smash you. (*A beat.*) I must go back in. The NKVD time toilet breaks. Tell your master. Comrade Stalin is willing to meet him, privately, later tonight.

ARCHIE. Churchill won't agree.

MOLOTOV. He must. I have imagined Hitler's victory parade in Red Square, after he has blown up Lenin's tomb. Can you imagine it in Whitehall, after he has blown up your memorial, what is it called?

ARCHIE. Cenotaph, the Cenotaph. (*A beat.*) I will try.

MOLOTOV. Try is not enough for us. Victory or death, my friend, victory or death.

He exits, shambling a little, checking his flies. ARCHIE *again alone on the stage.*

A blackout.

Interval.

Scene Six: 'Soviet Dust'

Corridor in the Kremlin. A huge chunky sofa. Enter OLGA *and* SALLY, *exhausted.*

SALLY. English or Russian?

OLGA. Please, English.

SALLY. It should be Russian, in your country...

OLGA. No no. It will be very good to hear English that is not... (*A shrug, a little smile.*)

SALLY. Churchillian?

OLGA. Oratorical?... (*A gesture.*)

SALLY. Oratorical, very good.

OLGA. Meaning 'blown-up'? But he is a great man, please do not think I am being rude.

SALLY. Not at all, and the Prime Minister does like blowing up.

OLGA. What of the Comrade General Secretary's Russian? He is oratorical?

SALLY. He comes across more as... gruff.

OLGA. Gruff. Yes. No-nonsense. That is him.

SALLY. He is a great man.

OLGA. Of course. (*A beat.*) My feet are murderous.

SALLY. 'Killing me.'

OLGA. Yes. Dead.

SALLY *smiles. They flop down on the sofa.*

Dust rises.

SALLY. Ooh, dust!

OLGA. It is an old sofa.

SALLY. It can't have been cleaned for years.

OLGA. It does not matter. People have no time to sit down in the Kremlin.

SALLY. You mean we could be the first ever to sit here?

OLGA (*laughs*). Why not? No more talks tonight, our work is done. We deserve it.

SALLY. You can bloody say that again.

SALLY *takes her shoes off and begins to massage her feet,* OLGA *watches then decides to follow* SALLY*'s example.*

I am knackered.

OLGA. 'Knackered.' Meaning 'pooped'.

SALLY. Pooped, right!

OLGA. It is slang? American?

SALLY. It was English. When old sailing ships had poops, a high deck, and the ships capsized and sank. And if you were standing on the poop you... (*She shrugs.*)

OLGA. So, we capsize and sink in sofa dust!

SALLY (*laughs*). We do.

A pause.

OLGA. 'Knackered' is a very noisy word.

SALLY. Yes! You can hear bones cracking inside it.

OLGA. To be sent to the knacker's yard. Where old animals are put to death.

SALLY. What would you say in Russian?

OLGA (*thinks for a moment*). Дойти до ручки. (*Transliteration: dayti da ruchki.*)

SALLY (*laughs*). Yes. (*A beat.*) Дойти до ручки. 'To reach the handle.' Means 'reaching rock bottom', I know, but why 'handle'?

OLGA. Oh, it's the old Russian traditional bread, the handle's the part different people touch as the loaf's passed person to person so it is dirty. You give the handle to the dogs.

SALLY. Or to the translators.

OLGA. Pooped, capsized, drowning, bones ground up, given to the dogs, that is us, but 'job done', yes?

SALLY. Thank God.

OLGA. I'm Olga.

SALLY. I'm Sally.

They shake hands then lie back relaxing, wiggling their feet for a while.

So... General Secretary Stalin has a dog called Tishka.

OLGA. And Prime Minister Churchill has a dog called Jock.

SALLY. Well, actually Jock's... never mind. (*She hesitates but she cannot hold it in.*) What I don't understand is... I mean... How can they, how can they, put so much away?

OLGA. Put away?

SALLY *with her hand, a drinking gesture.*

Ah! (*She laughs.*) Some admire vast alcohol consumption. It is seen as manly.

SALLY. I don't know why.

OLGA. It is a desire to be the last one standing.

SALLY. Maybe it's not that at all. Maybe they are scared.

OLGA (*shuts her down*). Comrade Stalin is not scared.

SALLY. No no of course not.

OLGA. Leaders have no fear. That is why we need them.

SALLY. I think they need to be as scared as we are. But know how to deal with it.

OLGA. You think Winston Churchill is scared?

SALLY. I bloody well hope he is.

OLGA. I do not understand. Why do you want him to be scared?

SALLY. So he knows what we're feeling.

OLGA. That is not what leaders are for.

SALLY. If they're not scared, it probably means they're mad. And will end up killing us all.

OLGA. This is incorrect thinking.

A silence.

Then they turn to each other.

SALLY. Look I...

OLGA. Yes forgive me, I think we have a chronic misunderstanding. Wrong end of stick?

SALLY. It's the translator's nightmare, the chronically wrong end of sticks.

OLGA. Confusing yes with no...

SALLY. No with yes...

They laugh.

A pause.

OLGA. I think the drinking is... warfare by other means.

SALLY. That's Clausewitz!

OLGA. Yes.

SALLY. Well, if the banquet was meant to... replace guns by vodka bottles, it was a disaster, the opposite seemed to happen. The atmosphere just got worse and worse.

OLGA. That's because... No.

SALLY. What?

OLGA. No one was speaking about... what they were speaking about.

SALLY. You mean the elephant in the room?

OLGA. As Dostoevsky wrote! You know the passage in *The Devils*?

SALLY. Yes, it's brilliant.

OLGA. What lies beneath. The untranslatable.

SALLY. Absolutely.

OLGA. Language is about what is not said.

SALLY. Yes.

OLGA (*'raising a glass' gesture*). 'To Rover.'

SALLY. 'To Ivan.' (*'Raising a glass' gesture.*)

OLGA. And may your dog choke on its bone. (*As if throwing the glass away.*)

SALLY. And yours upon its handle. (*As if throwing the glass away.*)

They laugh.

But translators are meant to be windows, aren't we, language windows, through which our countries can see each other clearly. We're not there to do the subtext. Put in stained glass. Colour things.

OLGA. But we look through the window and see what is meant, in ways they don't.

SALLY. I know, it's scary. (*A beat.*) Clausewitz. 'War is politics by other means.' An ugly thought.

OLGA. Truths are ugly.

SALLY. That's gloomy.

OLGA. Oh Russians love the gloom, the deeper the better, it's the winters. Making dreams of spring brighter.

They laugh.

SALLY. Your English, it's frightfully good. Where did you study?

OLGA. Here in Moscow.

SALLY. The Lomonosov University?

OLGA. For a while, then a special school.

SALLY. For translators?

OLGA (*sliding away from that*). Your Russian is excellent too, where did you...

SALLY. Cambridge. And a Foreign Office course.

OLGA. Ah.

Pause.

Have you been to Moscow before?

SALLY. First time. The Prime Minister wanted to bring someone new. How about you and London?

OLGA. No.

SALLY. I've dreamt of Moscow.

OLGA. And I of London.

SALLY. Or are we just saying that?

OLGA *looks at her.*

OLGA. We mean it. If the war is lost both our cities will no longer exist. Not in the way we love them.

SALLY. No. And we'll be dead.

OLGA. That is a certainty.

They are looking at each other. Are they about to touch each other's hands?

But SVETLANA *enters, running. She is carrying* David Copperfield. *She stops dead when she sees* SALLY *and* OLGA.

OLGA *goes rigid.* SALLY *smiles.*

SALLY. Добрый вечер, можем ли мы вам помочь? (*Transliteration: 'Dobryy vecher, mozhem li my vam pomoch?' Meaning 'Good evening, can we help you?'*)

SVETLANA *stares at her. Then turns, runs and exits.*

OLGA *is very concerned.*

Who was that?

OLGA. No one at all.

SALLY. It was... His daughter...

OLGA. No...

SALLY. Svetlana, there was the photo of her with her father in *Pravda*... I'd so love to talk to her...

OLGA. You are mistaken. It was a secretary. No one.

SALLY understands. A beat.

SALLY. No.

OLGA. There are many people, coming and going here.

SALLY. Of course.

OLGA (*lower*). Here, it is important for us to be discreet.

SALLY (*low*). I do understand.

A silence.

OLGA (*brightly*). I have a confession.

SALLY. Oh?

OLGA. It is terrible, may I share it?

SALLY. Er...

OLGA. The men haven't put me off. I am dying for a drink.

SALLY. Oh please!

OLGA. When does your plane leave?

SALLY. They said early morning...

OLGA. Then there is still time! We can go out.

SALLY. Isn't it too late?

OLGA. Everything is possible in Moscow at night. We are literary women! I am a member of the Writers' Union and the bar there never closes. Yes? I think the phrase is 'a quick one'?

SALLY. I'm your girl.

They are pulling their shoes on.

Enter MOLOTOV *and* ARCHIE, *brisk, tense. They gesture to speak to the translators.*

MOLOTOV. Comrade Dovzhenko!

ARCHIE. Lieutenant Powell!

They hurriedly get their shoes on. OLGA *and* MOLOTOV *go upstage to talk. We hear* SALLY *and* ARCHIE.

Stalin has invited him to meet in his private apartments. I've got him to agree.

SALLY. In the morning? So the talks are back on...

ARCHIE. Stalin wants to meet now. No officials, just you translators.

SALLY. Oh.

ARCHIE. If Winston... (*He pauses.*) I am going to be frank with you, Sally. (*Glances at* OLGA, *being briefed by* MOLOTOV.) We in the Embassy are desperately worried about... the Prime Minister's... grip on things.

SALLY. Sir?

ARCHIE. You'll be the only one of us in the room. You understand what I'm saying?

SALLY. I don't have any power...

ARCHIE. Oh you do. You are the words.

SALLY. You want me to edit what Stalin says? So the Prime Minister won't...

ARCHIE. I just want you to do your job, Lieutenant. Get the translation right.

SALLY. I hope –

ARCHIE. I mean right for us. You understand? (*Before she can reply.*) Good.

He walks away. She turns, furious. OLGA *and* MOLOTOV *come forward.*

MOLOTOV. One more thing.

OLGA. Yes, Comrade?

MOLOTOV. If you have the chance to speak to Churchill directly, you know your duty.

OLGA. I don't think…

MOLOTOV. I am going to share a vital piece of state intelligence. You will never reveal you heard this.

OLGA. Of course not, Comrade.

MOLOTOV. Churchill is thinking of making peace with Germany.

OLGA *is shocked.*

(*Low.*) Olga, you've seen what the man is, a brute, an aristo imperialist, an enemy of Socialism. For all his anti-Hitlerite posturing, he will turn against us. So. Anything. Any small clarification you have the chance to make, do it. Keep them in the room.

OLGA. Absolutely, Comrade Commissar.

SVETLANA *enters reading* David Copperfield. *She crouches down. Mouthing the words. She stops, thinking. She flicks through the pages. She reads from Chapter XIII.*

SVETLANA. 'My aunt, to my great alarm, became in one moment rigid with indignation, and had hardly voice to cry out, "Janet! Donkeys!"

Upon which, Janet came running up the stairs as if the house were in flames, darted out on a little piece of green in front, and warned off two saddle-donkeys, lady-ridden, that had presumed to set hoof upon it; while my aunt, rushing out of the house, seized the bridle of a third animal laden with a bestriding child, turned him, led him forth from those sacred precincts, and boxed the ears of the unlucky urchin in attendance who had dared to profane that hallowed ground…'

She smiles. She stops reading. She closes the book and walks away.

Scene Seven: 'Sweet Weapons'

A room in STALIN's *apartments. A low table with many bottles upon it. Two leather sofas behind it at a slight angle to each other.*

SALLY *and* OLGA *stand behind the sofas, stooping at times to whisper their translations.*

CHURCHILL. Thank you for this... most unexpected invitation.

OLGA (*translates*).

STALIN. Time for the real drink after the drink.

SALLY (*translates*).

Next six exchanges without translation.

CHURCHILL. Ah.

STALIN. Ah!

CHURCHILL. Yes.

STALIN. Da.

CHURCHILL. Da.

STALIN. Yes.

They look at each other. OLGA *and* SALLY *shrug.*

(*Calls out.*) Little Hostess, come to Papa!

CHURCHILL (*to* SALLY). What?

SALLY. A hostess –

Enter SVETLANA.

CHURCHILL *struggles to his feet.*

STALIN *stands, all smiles and graciousness.*

STALIN. Mr Prime Minister, this is my daughter Svetlana.

SALLY (*translates*).

CHURCHILL. Delighted, delighted.

SVETLANA (*good English, slightly accented*). Welcome to Moscow, Mr Prime Minister.

CHURCHILL. Enchanted to meet you, Miss Stalin.

SVETLANA. Thank you, sir.

She looks at STALIN, *who nods, smiling.*

Will you write in my book?

CHURCHILL. Delighted to.

She holds the book out. CHURCHILL *is lost for a pen,* SALLY *hands him one.* CHURCHILL *looks at the book and is surprised.*

David Copperfield, in English?

SVETLANA. Dickens is my favourite writer.

CHURCHILL. Ah, and what do you, ah, like about *Copperfield*?

SVETLANA. David's journey through life. To learn from experience.

CHURCHILL. A hard lesson.

STALIN *intervenes.*

STALIN. Our hostess has something for us to eat.

SALLY *hesitates but* SVETLANA *translates at once.*

SVETLANA. My father says would you like something to eat?

CHURCHILL. A little supper top-up would be very welcome.

SVETLANA. I will go and prepare it.

CHURCHILL. Most thoughtful of you, my dear. And here...

He writes in the book and gives it to her. STALIN *beams.*

SVETLANA. Thank you, Mr Churchill.

She exits.

CHURCHILL (*to* SALLY). The daughter, trying to make himself look human d'you think?

SALLY (*low*). I don't know, sir.

CHURCHILL. Hunh.

STALIN (*to* OLGA). Did you catch that?

OLGA (*low*). Something about... you being human.

STALIN. Hunh.

CHURCHILL. Your daughter is a delight.

OLGA (*translates*).

STALIN (*ignores that, pouring drinks*). Do you know what today is?

SALLY (*translates*).

CHURCHILL. Day? No. What, last of? Has the trumpet sounded?

OLGA (*translates*).

STALIN (*interrupting* OLGA). It is Napoleon's birthday.

SALLY (*translates*).

CHURCHILL. Napoleon! Annoying little man. Caused much trouble to your country and to mine.

OLGA (*translates*).

STALIN. But he stabilised the French Revolution. He was a great enemy.

SALLY (*translates*).

CHURCHILL. Generous of you. Since the bastard damn well burnt down Moscow!

OLGA (*translates*).

STALIN. No, we burnt down Moscow. Made the city useless to him. Scorched-earth tactic! Another great Russian invention. (*Twinkle of the eye.*) Like the telephone.

SALLY (*translates*).

CHURCHILL. Strange how every country claims to have invented the telephone. Even the Italians.

OLGA (*translates*).

STALIN *laughs*.

STALIN (*laughs*). Yes.

CHURCHILL. And when Moscow was burnt, the annoying little frog turned tail, retreated and you – (*A gesture.*) cut...

STALIN *looks at* OLGA.

OLGA (*translates*).

STALIN. Cut!

CHURCHILL. Cut his troops to bits!

STALIN. Da!

They are looking at each other intently. SALLY *and* OLGA *are uncertain.*

A pause, then CHURCHILL *speaks.*

CHURCHILL. And now that Hitler's fascist army has invaded, the Russian people have to do it all over again.

OLGA (*translates*).

CHURCHILL *shifts in his chair to lean forward, mustering all his earnestness.*

CHURCHILL. Mr General Secretary, the British nation knows very well of your great nation's history and indomitable spirit. And the peril you now face.

OLGA (*translates*).

STALIN. And, Prime Minister, I know very well of the sufferings of the British people in the Nazi bombings of your island. (*Raises his glass.*) To the confusion of our enemies!

SALLY (*translates*).

CHURCHILL (*raises his glass*). Confusion to them!

They drink.

STALIN. Where do I go now?

OLGA. Comrade?

STALIN. I know! (*To* CHURCHILL.) Your ancestor. I admire him.

SALLY (*translates*).

CHURCHILL. But which one? I have whole corridors of ancestors. Huge men in dark and gleaming armour in huge paintings on huge horses, along with their duchesses, heads of feathers, death-white shoulders, vast satin dresses. (*Sinking to reverie.*) The gloom of the house. The endless rainy afternoons. The lake through the windows like a sheet of lead. A mother dreaming of another country, sitting in an electric-blue ball gown by a rainy window. A father behind locked doors, locked in rage. In the nursery, tin soldiers, dead still across the carpet, fighting Waterloos forever. A little boy living with history. Yes.

OLGA (*translates, though getting lost*).

STALIN (*low to* OLGA). What the hell is he talking about?

OLGA (*low*). I think... about being brought up in a palace, Comrade.

STALIN. Ah. Blenheim.

CHURCHILL *springs back to life.*

CHURCHILL. Blenheim!

STALIN. Marlborough!

CHURCHILL. Ah! The Great Duke! My great-great-great-great-grandfather. Da!

STALIN. Great! Da! Great General! Marlborough!

STALIN *raises a glass.*

CHURCHILL. Marlborough!

They drink.

A silence. Both men are looking at each other.

(*Low, to* SALLY.) Where do I go next?

SCENE SEVEN

SALLY (*low*). I can't say, sir...

STALIN (*low, to* OLGA). When is he going to talk about the convoys?

OLGA (*low*). I don't know, Comrade...

STALIN. Is he playing some kind of game? Does he think this is rugby balls at Eton College?

OLGA. I think... he's a little drunk.

STALIN. No no he's faking it. Like I am.

SALLY (*to* CHURCHILL). It may be he's a bit...

CHURCHILL (*to* SALLY). What, the worse for wear? No no he's faking it. Like I am. Ah! I know where I'll go. (*To* STALIN.) Tell me...

OLGA (*translates*).

CHURCHILL. Tell me...

A silence.

OLGA (*translates*).

CHURCHILL. Tell me about Stalin's organ grinder.

OLGA (*translates*).

A silence.

STALIN. Do you mean the Katyusha rocket launcher?

SALLY (*translates*).

CHURCHILL. It is much admired by the British and American Allied High Command.

OLGA (*translates*).

STALIN. It's a very sweet weapon.

SALLY (*translates*).

CHURCHILL. Multiple rockets, mounted on a lorry, mobile, forty-eight rockets fired in, what, under a minute?

OLGA (*translates*).

STALIN. No no no! The Katyusha can fire a complete salvo in ten seconds!

SALLY (*translates*).

CHURCHILL. Forty-eight rockets in ten seconds. Sweet indeed.

OLGA (*translates*).

CHURCHILL. Though highly inaccurate, no?

OLGA (*translates*).

STALIN. Ha! Yes, yes, far less accurate than conventional artillery. But that is why it is feared.

SALLY (*translates*).

CHURCHILL. Ah. A weapon must be feared.

OLGA (*translates*).

STALIN. I am a great admirer of the British Army mortar. It is wonderfully inaccurate.

SALLY (*translates*).

CHURCHILL. Yes, terrifyingly so! Ah, the old Stokes three-inch. An old friend from the first war.

OLGA (*translates*).

STALIN. No. I mean your new two-inch mortar. That does not need a crew. One man... firing from the shoulder... (*He mimes lifting a mortar to his shoulder.*) Bang!

SALLY (*translates*).

CHURCHILL (*interrupts her*). I got that. The two-inch! Yes.

OLGA (*translates*).

STALIN. Maybe it should be given a name, like the Katyusha. Call it 'Churchill's Cigar'!

SALLY (*translates*).

CHURCHILL (*laughs, raises his cigar*). Ah. Bang!

CHURCHILL *and* STALIN *laugh.*

General Secretary, to come to substantive matters...

But enter, fast, a serious-looking MOLOTOV, *who interrupts.*

MOLOTOV (*low*). Comrade.

STALIN *turns on him in a fury.*

STALIN. What!? What!?

They look at each other. A silence. All still. Then STALIN *stands abruptly.*

(*To* CHURCHILL.) Forgive the rudeness of underlings.

SALLY (*translates*).

CHURCHILL. Please...

STALIN *and* MOLOTOV *hurry out of the room.*
CHURCHILL, SALLY, OLGA *remain. An uneasy silence.*

(*Low. To* SALLY.) What do you think? Good or bad news?

SALLY. Bad, I fear, sir.

CHURCHILL. Thought we were through the small talk, about to get somewhere, then...

A pause.

Well, since the, ah, master of the house has absented himself, would you ladies care for a... (*A gesture at the bottles.*) snifter?

SALLY (*looks at* OLGA). I don't think...

OLGA. No thank you, sir.

CHURCHILL. Ah. (*A beat.*) Red Army?

OLGA. Yes, sir.

CHURCHILL. Please excuse my ignorance of your uniform markings... what is your rank?

OLGA. Lieutenant, sir.

CHURCHILL. Ah! Same as Sally here. (*A beat.*) And, ah, where do you come from in the Soviet Union?

OLGA. Tomsk, sir.

CHURCHILL. Siberia. The vastness.

OLGA. Yes, sir.

CHURCHILL. I have a mental picture of a natural wonder. Millions of trees.

OLGA. Yes, sir.

SALLY is uncomfortable for OLGA, who is totally composed.

CHURCHILL. Do you mind if I ask you a question, which I feel we should always ask, of each other and of ourselves, even in the darkest of times. When we have peace, what will you do?

OLGA. Look after the trees.

CHURCHILL is taken aback: is she being sarcastic?

CHURCHILL. Ah.

OLGA. I trained as a forester at the Lenin Agricultural Institute in Tomsk.

CHURCHILL. A forester! We have foresters at Blenheim of course, but not, ah, female ones.

OLGA. Could I ask you, sir, what will you do?

CHURCHILL. Ha! Paint pictures of trees, I s'pose. (*A paintbrush gesture.*) Yes. (*A beat.*) We must keep sight of it, you know. Peace.

OLGA. This is a great patriotic war for us, Prime Minister. We will win, whatever the cost.

CHURCHILL looks at her sharply. Is this genuine or is this propaganda?

CHURCHILL. Spoken like a soldier, Lieutenant.

OLGA. I speak as a Soviet woman, sir.

STALIN *enters*.

STALIN. I have serious news.

SALLY (*translates*).

CHURCHILL (*low*). Stalingrad?

OLGA *freezes*.

STALIN. Stalingrad.

CHURCHILL. Da.

STALIN. The German Sixth Army have broken through and are in the city's suburbs.

SALLY (*translates*).

CHURCHILL. The Hun at the gates.

OLGA (*translates*).

STALIN. Da. And… Nothing? Nothing?

They are staring at each other.

The question is, do you expect Russia to bleed to save your wretched little island and its filthy Empire, while you do nothing? No! No! No.

SALLY *hesitates*. OLGA *looks alarmed*.

CHURCHILL. What?

SALLY. It's – heavily idiomatic.

CHURCHILL. The gist, give me the gist!

SALLY. He says – our countries must bleed together.

CHURCHILL. He said – 'niet', no!

SALLY. No to surrender –

OLGA *has caught the mistranslating. She and* SALLY *lock eyes.*

CHURCHILL. Dear God in Heaven, I thought Hitler was the Devil incarnate, but at this moment I believe I am looking at the real thing!

OLGA *hesitates*.

STALIN. What? What's he say?

OLGA. Hitler is the Devil incarnate, we... (*Looking at* SALLY.) We must be resolute in common cause against him.

STALIN. That's shit! Shit! Churchillian platitudes! Nothing fucking concrete! Convoys of weapons! Where the fuck are they? You lying imperialist pig!

SALLY, *shocked*.

CHURCHILL. He lost his temper! What did he say?

STALIN. But. But. But. British bulldog British shit!

CHURCHILL. What's he saying now!

SALLY. But. He's saying 'but'.

CHURCHILL. But what?

SALLY. But without your help we cannot win.

A pause, SALLY *and* OLGA *looking at each other.*

A frozen moment.

Then CHURCHILL *and* STALIN *simultaneously point at each other.*

CHURCHILL. Mr General Secretary. We cannot leave this room until we agree. We must have iron backsides.

OLGA *pulls herself together and translates*.

STALIN. The question is... whose bum is of the hardest iron?

SALLY (*translates*).

STALIN *and* CHURCHILL *are still pointing at each other.*

Then both men laugh. SALLY *and* OLGA *look at each other, relieved.*

Scene Eight: 'Powerless Corridor'

Kremlin corridor. The sofa.

ARCHIE, *pacing, talking to himself.*

ARCHIE. No agenda. Never go into a meeting without an agenda! (*Paces. Stops.*) And never have a meeting without having a meeting first about the meeting. (*Paces. Stops.*) Jesus Christ! We're trying to save civilisation. And there is no paperwork!

Paces.

Enter SVETLANA, *pushing a huge silver bomb dinner trolley, the lid closed. It clanks and rattles.*

SVETLANA (*English*). Have you read *David Copperfield*?

ARCHIE. What?

SVETLANA. It's a novel by Charles Dickens.

ARCHIE. Yes, yes so it is. Miss Stalin, forgive me, I was…

SVETLANA. I think he learns by experience, but that's just in a book.

ARCHIE. Indeed, yes. What is…

SVETLANA. Father ordered extra supper.

ARCHIE. Ah. Good…

SVETLANA. It must not get cold, excuse me please, Mr Ambassador.

ARCHIE. Yes, of course…

She exits, pushing the trolley.

They're out of control. Oh God.

Enter MOLOTOV.

They have ordered more food.

MOLOTOV. Well, a good sign.

ARCHIE. Is it?

MOLOTOV. As long as they are in the room, there is hope. You know what they called us Bolsheviks, in the days leading up to the Revolution?

ARCHIE. I...

MOLOTOV. 'Iron rumps.' Because we would never leave a meeting. Until we got what we wanted of course, then we'd walk out! And put those left behind on a list. (*He laughs*.)

ARCHIE. I am not finding this reassuring.

MOLOTOV. No no, forgive me. Old lags' tales.

He too is exhausted. He pinches the bridge of his nose.

ARCHIE. So... the situation in Stalingrad... you have new reports?

MOLOTOV. There is hand-to-hand fighting, building to building. We are holding the line to the west of the river. But if the Germans cross... (*He shrugs*.)

ARCHIE. Cross the Volga...

MOLOTOV. Yes yes.

ARCHIE. And you have told the General Secretary...

MOLOTOV (*irritated*). Of course!

ARCHIE. And he will have told the Prime Minister how serious it is?

MOLOTOV. I do not know, I cannot hear through walls!

ARCHIE (*low*). You can with the right equipment.

MOLOTOV. Forgive me?

ARCHIE *collects himself and returns to the attack.*

ARCHIE. It is essential that the Prime Minister know the military situation!

MOLOTOV. I'm sure the General Secretary will have informed him.

ARCHIE. But...

MOLOTOV. But what, Mr Ambassador?

They stare at each other other.

ARCHIE. We are both servants of unpredictable masters.

MOLOTOV. Stalin is not unpredictable, he acts according to the principles of dialectical materialism, to the inevitable demands of a scientific view of history.

ARCHIE. God, man, you believe that – crap?

MOLOTOV. I believe it absolutely. We are creatures of iron laws. The difference between the two men you call our masters is that Stalin knows it, Churchill does not.

ARCHIE. This is so dangerous.

MOLOTOV. On that, we agree.

They pace.

ARCHIE. We must go in there.

MOLOTOV. Not a good idea.

ARCHIE. Why not? It will offend iron laws?

MOLOTOV (*a light gesture*). More offend my chance of being alive in the morning.

ARCHIE *thinks this a joke but then realises he is serious.*

ARCHIE. What times are we living in?

MOLOTOV. My friend, in the heart of Moscow, tonight, at this moment in this war, it is unwise to assume we are alive at all.

Enter SALLY *and* OLGA. *They stop when they see* MOLOTOV *and* ARCHIE.

ARCHIE. Lieutenant!

MOLOTOV. Lieutenant!

ARCHIE. Why aren't you...

OLGA. We're dismissed!

SALLY (*to* ARCHIE). They don't want us in there.

OLGA (*to* MOLOTOV). Comrade Stalin told us to leave.

SALLY. The Prime Minister too. He said we were in the way.

A pause.

ARCHIE. So what are they doing in there?

OLGA. They eat pig.

SALLY. It's a roast suckling pig. Stalin's daughter brought it in.

ARCHIE. So they're just sitting there eating?

SALLY. No they're talking too.

ARCHIE. But Winston doesn't know a word of Russian and Stalin certainly has no English ...

MOLOTOV (*to* ARCHIE). They're talking without translation.

SALLY. It doesn't seem to bother them.

MOLOTOV. I must make a telephone call.

ARCHIE. I too, but...

MOLOTOV. If you wish a line to London, it will be secure.

ARCHIE *hesitates*.

You can be sure of that.

ARCHIE. Do I have a choice? (*To* SALLY.) Lieutenant, wait here. You may be needed.

SALLY. Yes, sir.

MOLOTOV (*to* OLGA). You are still on duty.

OLGA. Yes, Comrade.

MOLOTOV *and* ARCHIE *exit at speed*.

I am beyond pooped.

SALLY. I've got the handle, good and proper.

OLGA. Correct usage!

SALLY. Thank you, miss. (*A pause*.) What happened in there?

OLGA. I don't know.

SALLY. It scared me...

OLGA. It began with them chewing the pig and grunting, yes?

SALLY. Yes, grunts.

OLGA. Then the joke when they broke wind.

SALLY (*grimace*). The smell in there, with the meat...

OLGA. I think... they have found the language of the common mind.

SALLY. Farting?

OLGA. I am serious. There is a Soviet theory of linguistics. It says there is, at root, only one language, out of the common mind of humanity, whatever the class or culture or country of the speaker.

SALLY. That sounds utterly crackpot.

OLGA. It was in an article in *Pravda*, written by Comrade Stalin.

SALLY. Whoops. Still, it is a bit... mystical...?

OLGA (*smiles*). You mean for a Communist?

SALLY. Well, yes.

OLGA. Not at all.

A pause.

SALLY. We... mistranslated.

OLGA. No. They heard what they had to.

SALLY. I feel I've... betrayed something.

OLGA. Betrayed what?

SALLY. Truth.

OLGA. Victory is all that matters. Win and everything is true.

SALLY. I don't understand that.

OLGA. That's why, in the end, you will lose.

SALLY. Me? Lose?

OLGA. The West.

SALLY. Ah.

A pause.

You are NKVD.

OLGA. You are MI6.

SALLY. I was briefed you would be.

OLGA. I was briefed about you.

A pause.

SALLY. So. We are true believers.

OLGA. It would seem so, Sally.

SALLY. I love Russian.

OLGA. I love English too.

SALLY. Russian goes deep.

OLGA. English goes all over the place.

They laugh.

The languages love each other.

SALLY. But I don't think we're like those old men in there. Not at all.

OLGA. They are our leaders. The best of us.

SALLY. Are they?

Scene Nine: 'World Imperial'

CHURCHILL *and* STALIN. *Before them, on a low table, there is a whole roast hog, much cut and torn into. The meat glistens. Both have knives they use to cut meat. Many opened bottles.*

They are eating.

Gestures, grunts, full mouths.

Note: in the scene they begin to understand what each other is saying at first by charade-like gestures, then by a kind of osmosis. Their inner monologues entwine.

STALIN. We...

CHURCHILL. You?

STALIN (*shakes his head*). We...

CHURCHILL. Ah, you, meaning we... (*Meaning the two of them.*)

STALIN (*shakes his head*). No. We...

CHURCHILL. Ah, we, you, Russian people?

STALIN. Soviet.

CHURCHILL. Soviet, Russian, same thing...

STALIN (*finger wagging*). No no no, not, Soviet man new, Soviet woman new...

CHURCHILL. Yes yes, you, the Soviet people...

    STALIN *points down at the floor, vigorously.*

Down?

    STALIN *makes spade digging motions.*

(*Copying the gestures.*) Plant, dig...

STALIN. Niet. (*Points to himself.*) Will... (*Points down.*) You. (*Makes slapping down a spade motions.*)

    A beat.

We... will bury... you.

They stare at each other.

CHURCHILL. We will bury *you*.

A pause. They reach for glasses, chink them and drink.

Julius Caesar.

STALIN. Caesar.

CHURCHILL. Scorched earth.

STALIN. Caesar. Da.

CHURCHILL. What you fight now.

STALIN. Julius Caesar!

CHURCHILL. Julius Caesar!

A pause. Then their faces crease into grins and they laugh. They chink glasses and drink.

History.

STALIN. History.

CHURCHILL *mimes putting a burden across his shoulder.*

CHURCHILL. Yoke.

STALIN. Yoke?

CHURCHILL *mimes being weighed down.*

CHURCHILL. I feel the weight.

STALIN. If you are saying you feel the weight, I don't.

CHURCHILL. There is an enemy within. (*Thumps his chest.*)

STALIN. If you mean an 'enemy within', night thoughts, black dogs...

CHURCHILL. It is a black dog, some nights, by the bed, long hours...

STALIN. Dogs!

CHURCHILL. Dogs! (*Thumps his chest again.*)

STALIN (*shakes his head, wagging his finger*). My dogs are not within. They are the plotters, the other side of doors. (*He tries to communicate this. Thick accent.*) Julius Caesar!

CHURCHILL. Caesar again!

STALIN *mimes stabbing and points to his back.*

Yes, murdered on the Capitol, et tu Brute.

STALIN. Brutuses. Many.

CHURCHILL. You face opposition?

STALIN. Plotters. (*He makes a 'gun shooting in the head' gesture.*)

CHURCHILL. Ah. No need to shoot opponents in England. We send 'em to the House of Lords.

He laughs. STALIN *has not gathered why but he laughs with him. They drink.*

And your Kulaks?

STALIN *looks at him and shrugs.*

STALIN. Kulaks?

CHURCHILL. The peasants. When you threw them off their farms.

STALIN s*hakes his head, not understanding.*

When the State collectivised the land?

STALIN. Ah…! Collectivisation! Yes. Soviet triumph! (*Another shrug, questioning: What do you want to know?*)

CHURCHILL. Where did they… (*A dispersal gesture.*) go? The Kulaks?

STALIN. They… (*The same dispersal gesture.*) went away.

CHURCHILL. Ten million of them?

STALIN *is unmoved. A silence.*

STALIN. The British in India.

CHURCHILL. India?

STALIN. After the mutiny.

CHURCHILL. India. Ah.

STALIN. In punishment actions after the mutiny, how many did the British kill... (*A sweeping gesture.*) All across the subcontinent? (*Fingers held up.*) Seven? Eight million?

CHURCHILL. Ah.

CHURCHILL *is unmoved. A silence.*

Now we would discuss necessity, if we could really follow, follow each other. (*A beat.*) But maybe we do.

Monologues entwining.

STALIN. No choice.

CHURCHILL. For there's no choice, is there.

STALIN. We needed more food. For workers in the new industries.

CHURCHILL. India, trade, the Victorians had no choice, open the East or the West would perish.

STALIN. India? Ha! Karl Marx said better the British occupy it than the Russians or the Turks!

CHURCHILL. Black and Tans.

STALIN. Trotsky and all the others.

CHURCHILL. Bomb Iraq, 1914. Hundred thousand Arabs dead. My orders.

STALIN. My order number two-two-seven, sent tonight: 'Kill the cowards.'

CHURCHILL. Famine in India coming? Ignore.

STALIN. Gulag. Ignore.

CHURCHILL (*finger to his mouth*). Sh!

STALIN (*finger to his mouth*). Sh!

SCENE NINE 79

CHURCHILL. Brutal truths.

STALIN. Brutal truths.

CHURCHILL. Say it not on the Clapham omnibus, say it not in the voting booth, but without force no civilisation.

STALIN. Speak of freedom, practise order.

CHURCHILL. Force.

STALIN. Force.

They re-engage and understand each other more.

CHURCHILL. Ah! Omelette?

STALIN. Omelette?

CHURCHILL. Eggs. (*Mimes cracking.*)

STALIN. The old cliché, can't make an omelette without breaking eggs.

CHURCHILL. Lenin said?

STALIN. Not Lenin.

CHURCHILL. No?

STALIN. Robespierre.

CHURCHILL. Ah.

STALIN. Great man.

CHURCHILL. Well... I suppose he had his moments.

They go into monologue mode, not looking at each other.

Power. The mystery of it, there then gone.

STALIN. Robespierre lost power the moment... they laughed at him. Then he was nothing. A feeble creature with his jaw shot away, carried to a guillotine.

CHURCHILL. We assume command flows from us. From this room.

STALIN. Never let them laugh at you. Keep them afraid. Fill every space with you, in public, in their heads.

CHURCHILL. Secretaries in the corridors waiting, telephones, telegraph machines at the ready…

STALIN. Always be still. On the posters, in the statues, looking toward horizons.

CHURCHILL. We assume command flows.

STALIN. In newsreels, always walk forward, never look aside.

CHURCHILL. They wait tonight, the ships, the planes, the men and women, all the men and women, in the ministries…

STALIN. So… you are them, they are you, you are the body of the nation, embody, yes, you embody their lives, you are their lives… so tonight the orders are as one. The will is as one.

CHURCHILL. All the brave souls aboard the ships, convoys waiting in Scapa Flow, fighters on the South Downs airfields, men in the oil-stinking tanks in the desert, they wait. For my voice. That comes from this room. Tonight.

STALIN. Power is overwhelming fear, for the good.

CHURCHILL. Power is the democratic will, for the good.

STALIN. I was born to take it.

CHURCHILL. I was born to wield it.

STALIN. And I can lose it like…

Holds his hand up.

CHURCHILL. I can lose it like…

Holds his hand up.

STALIN *and* CHURCHILL *click their fingers together.*

And they are looking at each other, startled.

You cannot bury us.

They both know they have reached the crux of the meeting. They are watching each other intently.

STALIN. Nor…

CHURCHILL. No.

STALIN. You, us.

CHURCHILL. No.

A pause. They are now very alert.

Convoys.

STALIN. Convoys.

CHURCHILL. Whatever the cost.

STALIN. You send... convoys.

CHURCHILL. Whatever the cost.

STALIN. And two... (*Fingers held up. The 'mortar firing' gesture.*)

CHURCHILL. Yes, two-inch mortars...

STALIN. We will fight. In Stalingrad. We will fight.

CHURCHILL. We will fight.

STALIN. To the end.

CHURCHILL. In extremes, all is possible.

STALIN. Death or victory.

CHURCHILL. Death or victory.

They are leaning forward, as close to each other as they can be.

STALIN. You... (*Points at him.*) Empire. (*Points to himself.*) We... Socialist World.

CHURCHILL (*makes a round gesture*). Spheres of influence.

STALIN. Sphere... (*He makes the round sign.*) And after the war... (*A heavy chopping gesture with his hand through the sphere.*)

CHURCHILL. Yes! After the war.

STALIN. Coexist.

CHURCHILL. Coexist. East, West. Yes.

STALIN. We will meet... (*A gesture pushing his fists together.*)

CHURCHILL. In Germany.

STALIN. In Germany. (*Turns his fists into a handshake. Then he laughs and raises a glass.*) To our Empires!

CHURCHILL (*raises a glass. Laughs*). Our Empires! (*To himself.*) Whatever we secretly think.

STALIN (*to himself*). Whatever we secretly think.

They drink.

The Socialist World forever!

He throws the glass, it smashes.

CHURCHILL. The British Empire forever!

He throws the glass, it smashes. They stand lumbering together. Some bottles fall. They embrace. They fall onto STALIN*'s chair in each others arms.*

STALIN *and* CHURCHILL. Oooh! Ohh! Oooh!

They laugh.

Enter ARCHIE *and* MOLOTOV, *with* SALLY *and* OLGA. *They look appalled.*

STALIN (*looks up at* MOLOTOV). ******

SALLY (*translates*). We have a new world order.

CHURCHILL. ******

OLGA (*translates*). Together we stand.

STALIN *and* CHURCHILL *laugh.*

ARCHIE. I think we better...

MOLOTOV. Yes...

They are helping STALIN *and* CHURCHILL *to stand up.*

CHURCHILL. I understand him, Archie, I really do...

ARCHIE. Yes, sir, let's get you back to...

CHURCHILL. I think there are two Joe Stalins...

STALIN. What's he say?

OLGA. He thinks there are two of you.

STALIN. Let him think anything, as long as we fight on.

SALLY. He says...

CHURCHILL. No no. I've seen into the man's soul. He's seen into mine.

CHURCHILL *and* STALIN *stand to attention. They salute each other.*

Scene Ten: 'Svetlana Will'

SVETLANA *stands before the mess left by the late-night eating and drink.*

Then, in a fury, she attacks the remnants of the roast pig, throwing bits of meat and bone about her.

SVETLANA. I will!

I will!

Know how my mother died! Not peritonitis, she shot herself. During one of my father's late-night parties. He flirted with a woman. She went into her room and shot herself.

And I will know that. Later, but I will know it.

And I will fall in love. When I am seventeen.

With a Jewish student in Moscow.

And Father will forbid me marrying him and send him to a camp.

And Father will make me marry a brute. Son of Zhadanov, the censor, persecutor of artists.

And I will divorce him.

I will be an artist, I will write.

And Father will die. He will.

He will die and I will stand in the room and I will weep.

And I will fall in love with a man from India.

And he will be the love of my life.

And I will not be allowed to marry him.

And he will die.

And I will take his ashes to spread them upon the holy river of the Ganges.

And I will lose my atheism.

And I will see the many faces of God.

And I will go into the American Embassy in Delhi, and say who I am, Svetlana Stalin, and defect.

And I will live.

And I will see the fall of empires. In my lifetime, no more Soviet Union, no more British Empire.

I will live.

I will gain experience.

I will be me.

End of play.

A Nick Hern Book

Churchill in Moscow first published as a paperback original in Great Britain in 2025 by Nick Hern Books Limited, The Glasshouse, 49a Goldhawk Road, London W12 8QP, in association with the Orange Tree Theatre, London

Churchill in Moscow © 2025 Howard Brenton

Howard Brenton has asserted his right to be identified as the author of this work

Cover photography by Rebecca Need-Menear. Design by Annie Rushton

Designed and typeset by Nick Hern Books, London
Printed in Great Britain by Mimeo Ltd, Huntingdon, Cambridgeshire PE29 6XX

A CIP catalogue record for this book is available from the British Library

ISBN 978 1 83904 417 5

CAUTION All rights whatsoever in this play are strictly reserved. Requests to reproduce the text in whole or in part should be addressed to the publisher.

Amateur Performing Rights Applications for performance, including readings and excerpts, by amateurs in the English language throughout the world should be addressed to the Performing Rights Manager, Nick Hern Books, The Glasshouse, 49a Goldhawk Road, London W12 8QP, *tel* +44 (0)20 8749 4953, *email* rights@nickhernbooks.co.uk, except as follows:

Australia: ORiGiN Theatrical, *email* enquiries@originmusic.com.au, *web* www.origintheatrical.com.au

New Zealand: Play Bureau, 20 Rua Street, Mangapapa, Gisborne, 4010, *tel* +64 21 258 3998, *email* info@playbureau.com

USA and Canada: Casarotto Ramsay and Associates Ltd, see details below

Professional Performing Rights Applications for performance by professionals in any medium and in any language throughout the world (including by stock companies in the USA and Canada) should be addressed to Casarotto Ramsay and Associates Ltd, *email* rights@casarotto.co.uk, www.casarotto.co.uk

No performance of any kind may be given unless a licence has been obtained. Applications should be made before rehearsals begin. Publication of this play does not necessarily indicate its availability for amateur performance.

www.nickhernbooks.co.uk/environmental-policy

Nick Hern Books' authorised representative in the EU is
Easy Access System Europe – Mustamäe tee 50, 10621 Tallinn, Estonia
email gpsr.requests@easproject.com

www.nickhernbooks.co.uk

@nickhernbooks